13092322

Editors: Basil Meeking and John Stott

THE EVANGELICAL–ROMAN CATHOLIC DIALOGUE ON MISSION

1977–1984

A REPORT

BR
1641
.C37
E93
1986

WILLIAM B. EERDMANS PUBLISHING COMPANY

THE PATERNOSTER PRESS

Copyright © 1986 Basil Meeking and John Stott

All rights reserved. No part of this publication may
be reproduced, stored in a retrieval system, or
transmitted, in any form or by any means, electronic,
mechanical, photocopying, recording or otherwise,
without the prior permission of
THE PATERNOSTER PRESS

AUSTRALIA:
Bookhouse Australia Ltd.,
P.O. Box 115, Flemington Markets, NSW 2129

SOUTH AFRICA:
Oxford University Press,
P.O. Box 1141, Cape Town

British Library Cataloguing in Publication Data

The Evangelical - Roman Catholic dialogue on mission
1977–1984 : a report.
1. Missions
266   BV2061
ISBN 0-85364-437-3

Library of Congress Cataloguing in Publication Data

Evangelical-Roman Catholic Dialogue on Mission.
The Evangelical-Roman Catholic Dialogue on Mission,
1977–1984.

Report on the meetings held at Venice in 1977, Cambridge in
1982, and Landévennec, France in 1984.
Bibliography: p.
1. Evangelicalism—Relations—Catholic Church—Congresses.
2. Catholic Church—Relations—Evangelicalism—Congresses.
3. Missions—Theory—Congresses.
I. Stott, John R. W.   II. Meeking, Basil.   III. Title.
BR1641.C37E93   1986   266'.001   86–1977
ISBN 0–8028–0184–6 (pbk.)

Photoset in Great Britain by
Photoprint, 9–11 Alexandra Lane, Torquay, Devon
and printed for The Paternoster Press,
Paternoster House, 3 Mount Radford Crescent, Exeter, Devon
by A. Wheaton & Co., Ltd., Exeter

Contents

The Library
INTERNATIONAL CHRISTIAN
GRADUATE UNIVERSITY

43016

All scriptural references are taken from the RSV (*The Common Bible,* Collins 1973)

Participants

(For details of meetings attended, see pp. 93 and 94).

Evangelical Participants

Dr Kwame Bediako
Professor Peter Beyerhaus
Bishop Donald Cameron
Dr Harvie Conn
Dr Orlando Costas
Mr Martin Goldsmith
Dr David Hubbard
Rev. Gottfried Osei-Mensah
Rev. Peter Savage
Rev. John Stott
Dr David Wells

Roman Catholic Participants

Sister Joan Chatfield
Father Matthieu Collin
Sister Joan Delaney
Father Parmananda Divarkar
Father Pierre Duprey
Father Claude Geffré
Father René Girault
Monsignor Basil Meeking
Monsignor Jorge Mejia
Father Dionisio Minguez
  Fernandez
Father John Paul Musinsky
Father John Mutiso-Mbinda
Father Waly Neven
Father John Redford
Father Philip Rosato
Monsignor Pietro Rossano
Father Robert Rweyemamu
Bishop Anselme Sanon
Father Bernard Sesboué
Father Thomas Stransky

Introduction

The Evangelical-Roman Catholic Dialogue on Mission was a series of three meetings which took place over a period of seven years. The first was held at Venice in 1977, the second at Cambridge in 1982 and the third at Landévennec in France in 1984.

(i) The Participants

Those who took part in the dialogue were theologians and missiologists from many parts of the world. Their names are given on pages 7, 8, and 93, 94. Six of us (three from each side) attended all three meetings; others were able to come to only one or two of them.

The Evangelical participants were drawn from a number of churches and Christian organisations. They were not official representatives of any international body, however. For the evangelical movement has a broad spectrum, which includes evangelical denominations (both within and outside the World Council of Churches), evangelical fellowships (within mainline, comprehensive denominations), and evangelical parachurch agencies (specializing in tasks like Bible translation, evangelism,[1] cross-cultural mission, and Third World relief and development), which accept different degrees of responsibility to the Church.[2]

It is not easy to give a brief account of the distinctive beliefs of evangelical Christians, since different churches and groups emphasize different doctrines. Yet all Evangelicals share a cluster of theological convictions which were recovered and reaffirmed by the 16th century Reformers. These include (in addition to the great affirmations of the Nicene Creed) the inspiration and authority of the Bible, the sufficiency of its teaching for salvation, and its supremacy over the traditions of the Church; the justification of sinners (i.e. their acceptance by God as righteous in his sight) on the sole ground of the sinbearing—often called 'substitutionary'—death of Jesus Christ, by God's free grace alone, apprehended by faith alone, without the addition of any human works; the inward work of the Holy Spirit to bring about the new birth and to transform the regenerate into the likeness of Christ; the necessity of personal repentance and faith in Christ ('conversion'); the Church as the Body of Christ, which incorporates all true believers, and all of whose members are called to ministry, some being 'evangelists, pastors and teachers'; the 'priesthood of all believers', who (without any priestly mediation except Christ's) all enjoy equal access to God and all offer him their sacrifice of praise and worship; the urgency of the great commission to spread the gospel throughout the world, both verbally in proclamation and visually in good works of love; and the expectation of the personal, visible and glorious return of Jesus Christ to save, to reign and to judge.

The Roman Catholic participants, who spoke from the point of view of the official teaching of their Church, were named by the Vatican Secretariat for Promoting Christian Unity. The existence of the Secretariat is evidence of the effective renewal of attitude towards other Christians, which has taken place among Roman Catholics as a result of the Second Vatican Council twenty years ago, and which is still having its effects. In that Council it was acknowledged that 'Christ summons the Church, as she goes her pilgrim way, to that continual reformation of which she always has need, insofar as she is an institution of men here on earth'.[3] As a result, Roman Catholics have been able to acknowledge joyfully 'the riches of Christ and virtuous works in the lives of others who are bearing witness to Christ'.[4] This same renewal turned the attention of Roman Catholics to the Scriptures in a new way, exhorting the Church 'to move ahead daily towards a deeper understanding of the Sacred Scriptures' which 'contain the Word of God and, since they are inspired, really are that word'.[5] And it led to a better expression of the relation between Scripture and tradition in communicating God's Word in its full purity. Here indeed are the elements which have enabled Roman Catholics to acknowledge common ground with other Christians, and to assume their own responsibility for overcoming divisions for the sake of the mission of God and the fullness of his glory.

(ii) The Background

It is the will of God that 'all men be saved and come to the knowledge of the truth. For there is one God, and there is one mediator between God and men, the man Christ Jesus, who gave himself as a ransom for all' (1 Tim. 2:4–5); 'there is salvation in no one else' (Acts 4:12). Mission begins in the activity of God himself who sent his Son, and whose Son sent his Spirit. All who belong to God in Jesus Christ must share in this mission of God.

A dialogue on mission between Evangelicals and Roman Catholics has been possible for two reasons. First, both constituencies have recently been concentrating their attention on evangelism. In July 1974 the evangelical International Congress on World Evangelization took place in Switzerland and issued the 'Lausanne Covenant'.[6] A few months later the Third General Assembly of the Roman Catholic Synod of Bishops studied the same topic, and at their request Pope Paul VI issued in December 1975 his apostolic exhortation entitled *Evangelii Nuntiandi*, or 'Evangelization in the Modern World'.[7]

Secondly, a study of these two documents reveals a measure of convergence in our understanding of the nature of evangelism, as the following quotations show: 'To evangelize is to spread the

good news that Jesus Christ died for our sins and was raised from
the dead according to the Scriptures . . . Evangelism itself is the
proclamation of the historical, biblical Christ as Saviour and
Lord . . .'[8] Again, witness must be 'made explicit by a clear and
unequivocal proclamation of the Lord Jesus . . . There is no true
evangelization if the name, the teaching, the life, the promises,
the Kingdom and the mystery of Jesus of Nazareth, the Son of
God, are not proclaimed'.[9]

(iii) The Experience

In our time there are many possible forms of dialogue. Some are
undertaken with an immediate view to working for organic unity
between the bodies which the participants represent. Others do
not exclude this purpose, but begin from where they are with a
more general purpose. Still others begin by stating that they do
not envisage organic or structural unity but aim rather at an
exchange of theological views in order to increase mutual
understanding and to discover what theological ground they hold
in common. ERCDOM has been a dialogue of the latter kind. It
was not conceived as a step towards Church unity negotiations.
Rather it has been a search for such common ground as might be
discovered between Evangelicals and Roman Catholics as they
each try to be more faithful in their obedience to mission. It was
also undertaken quite consciously in the knowledge that there
are still both disagreements and misrepresentations between
Evangelicals and Roman Catholics which harm our witness to the
gospel, contradict our Lord's prayer for the unity of his
followers, and need if possible to be overcome.

During the three meetings friendships were formed, and
mutual respect and understanding grew, as the participants
learned to listen to one another and to grapple with difficult and
divisive questions, as well as rejoicing in the discovery of some
common understandings.

It was a demanding experience as well as a rewarding one. It
was marked by a will to speak the truth, plainly, without
equivocation, and in love. Neither compromise nor the quest for

lowest common denominators had a place; a patient search for truth and a respect for each other's integrity did.

(iv) The Report

This Report is in no sense an 'agreed statement', but rather a faithful record of the ideas shared. It is not exhaustive, for more questions were touched on than could be described in this brief compass. Yet enough has been included to give a substantial idea of how the dialogue developed and to communicate something of it without creating misunderstandings or false expectations.

An effort has been made to convey what went on at all three meetings, bearing in mind that in none was a complete exposé given of most issues. ERCDOM was only a first step, even if not a negligible one.

Our Report, as far as it goes, gives a description of some areas in which Evangelicals and Roman Catholics hold similar or common views, which we are able to perceive more clearly as we overcome the stereotypes and prejudiced ideas which we have of each other. In addition, it sets out some of the serious matters on which Evangelicals and Roman Catholics differ, but about which in the last seven years the participants in ERCDOM have begun to learn to speak and listen to each other.

Although all those who participated in the three meetings contributed richly, the responsibility for the final form of the Report rests with those who were at Landévennec. Publication is undertaken on the general endorsement of the 1984 participants, although it is not the kind of document to which each has asked to subscribe formally. Nevertheless it is their express hope that it may be a means of stimulating local encounters in dialogue between Evangelicals and Roman Catholics. Our Report is far from being definitive; the dialogue needs to be continued and developed.

The participants in ERCDOM offer this Report to other Evangelicals and Roman Catholics as a sign of their conviction that fidelity to Jesus Christ today requires that we take his will for his followers with a new seriousness. He prayed for the truth, holiness, mission and unity of his people. We believe that these dimensions of the Church's renewal belong together. It is with this understanding that we echo his prayer for ourselves and each other:

> 'Sanctify them in the truth; thy word is truth. As thou didst send me into the world, so I have sent them into the world . . . I pray . . . that they may all be one; even as thou, Father, art in me, and I in thee, that they also may be in us, so that the world may believe . . .' (Jn. 17:17–21).

1
Revelation and Authority

1

Revelation and Authority

It may well be asked why participants in a dialogue on mission should spend time debating theological questions concerned with divine revelation, the Scriptures, the formulation of truth, principles of biblical interpretation, and the church's *magisterium* or teaching authority. For these topics may not appear to be directly related to our Christian mission in the world. Yet we judged a discussion of them to be indispensable to our task, for two main reasons. The first and historical reason is that the issue of authority in general, and of the relation between Scripture and tradition in particular, was one of the really major points at issue in the 16th century. Indeed, the evangelical emphasis on *sola Scriptura* has always been known as the 'formal' principle of the Reformation. So Roman Catholics and Evangelicals will not come to closer understanding or agreement on *any* topic if they cannot do so on *this* topic. Indeed, in every branch of the Christian Church the old question 'by what authority?' (Mk. 11:28) remains fundamental to ecumenical discussion. Our second reason for including this subject on our agenda was that it has a greater relevance to mission than may at first appear. For there can be no mission without a message, no message without a definition of it, and no definition without agreement as to how, or on what basis, it shall be defined.

(i) Revelation, the Bible and the Formulation of Truth

Roman Catholics and Evangelicals are entirely agreed on the necessity of revelation, if human beings are ever to know God. For he is infinite in his perfections, while we are both finite creatures and fallen sinners. His thoughts and ways are as much higher than ours as the heavens are higher than the earth (Is. 55:9). He is beyond us, utterly unknowable unless he should choose to make himself known, and utterly unreachable unless he should put himself within our reach. And this is what together we believe he has done. He has revealed the glory of his power in the created universe,[10] and the glory of his grace in his Son Jesus Christ, and in the Scriptures which he said bear witness to him (e.g. John 5:39).

This process of special revelation began in the Old Testament era. 'God spoke of old to our fathers by the prophets' (Heb. 1:1). He fashioned Israel to be his people and taught them by his law and prophets. Old Testament Scripture records this history and this teaching. Then the Father sent his Son, who claimed to be the fulfilment of prophecy, himself proclaimed the good news of salvation, chose the twelve apostles to be his special witnesses, and promised them the inspiration of his Spirit. After Pentecost they went everywhere preaching the gospel. Through their word Christian communities came into being, nourished by the Old Testament and the gospel. The apostles' teaching was embodied in hymns, confessions of faith and particularly their letters. In due time the Church came to recognize their writings as possessing unique authority and as handing down the authentic gospel of Jesus Christ. In this way the canon of the New Testament was constituted, which with the Old Testament comprise the Christian Scriptures.

We all recognize that in the Scriptures God has used human words as the vehicle of his communication. The Spirit's work of inspiration is such, however, that what the human authors wrote is what God intended should be revealed, and thus that Scripture is without error. Because it is God's Word, its divine authority and unity must be recognized, and because he spoke through human beings, its original human context must also be taken into account in the work of interpretation.

But are human words adequate to describe God fully, even if they are inspired? No. The infinite reality of the living God is a mystery which cannot be fully communicated in words or fully comprehended by human minds. No verbal formulation can be co-extensive with the truth as it is in him. Nevertheless, God has condescended to use words as well as deeds as appropriate media of his self-disclosure, and we must struggle to understand them. We do so in the confidence, however, that though they do not reveal God fully, they do reveal him truly.

Roman Catholics and Evangelicals differ slightly in their understandings of the nature of Scripture, and even more on what the proper process of interpreting this Word should be. Both groups recognize that God spoke through the human authors, whose words belonged to particular cultures.

Roman Catholics speak of this relationship between the divine and the human in Scripture as being analogous to the divine and the human in Christ. As the Second Vatican Council put it, 'Indeed the words of God, expressed in the words of men, are in every way like human language, just as the Word of the eternal Father, when he took on himself the flesh of human weakness, became like man'.[11] Thus the written testimony of the biblical authors is inscribed within the logic of the Incarnation.

Evangelicals also sometimes use this analogy, but they are not altogether comfortable with it. Although it has some validity, they do not believe it is exact, since there is no hypostatic union between the human and the divine in Scripture. They usually emphasize instead the model of God's providence, namely that he is able even through fallen human beings to accomplish his perfect will. So he has spoken through the human authors of the Bible in such a way that neither did he suppress their personality nor did they distort his revelation.

Thus together we affirm that the written Word of God is the

work of both God and human beings. The divine and the human elements form a unity which cannot be torn asunder. It excludes all confusion and all separation between them.

With respect to the process of interpretation, Roman Catholics affirm that Scripture must be seen as having been produced by and within the Church. It is mediated to us by the inspired witness of the first Christians. The proper process of interpretation is determined by the process of Scripture's creation. We cannot understand it in its truth unless we receive it in the living faith of the Church which, assisted by the Holy Spirit, keeps us in obedience to the Word of God.

Evangelicals acknowledge the wisdom of listening to the Church and its teachers, past and present, as they seek to understand God's Word, but they insist that each believer must be free to exercise his or her personal responsibility before God, in hearing and obeying his Word. While the Church's interpretations are often helpful, they are not finally necessary because Scripture, under the Spirit's illumination, is self-interpreting and perspicuous (clear).

Thus, contemporaneity has come to mean different things in our two communities. Each recognizes that the Word of God must be heard for and in our world today. For Roman Catholics God's Word is contemporary in the sense that it is heard and interpreted within the living Church. For Evangelicals it is contemporary in the sense that its truth has to be applied, by the illumination of the Holy Spirit, to the modern world.

Despite these differences, we are agreed that since the biblical texts have been inspired by God, they remain the ultimate, permanent and normative reference of the revelation of God. To them the Church must continually return, in order to discern more clearly what they mean, and so receive fresh insight, challenge and reformation. They themselves do not need to be reformed, although they do need constantly to be interpreted, especially in circumstances in which the Church encounters new problems or different cultures. Roman Catholics hold that 'the task of giving an authentic interpretation of the Word of God whether in its written form or in the form of Tradition has been entrusted to the living, teaching office of the Church alone'.[12]

This seems to Evangelicals to derogate from Scripture as 'the ultimate, permanent and normative reference'. Nevertheless, both sides strongly affirm the divine inspiration of Scripture.

(ii) Principles of Biblical Interpretation

Our understanding of the nature of the Bible determines our interpretation of it. Because it is the Word of God, we shall approach it in one way; and because it is also the words of men, in another.

a. *Humble dependence on the Holy Spirit*

Because the Bible is the Word of God, we must approach it with reverence and humility. We cannot understand God's revelation by ourselves, because it is 'spiritually discerned' (1 Cor. 2:14). Only he who spoke through the prophets and apostles can interpret to us his own message. Only the Spirit of truth can open our hearts to understand, to believe and to obey. This is 'wisdom', and the Holy Spirit is the 'Spirit of wisdom and of revelation' in our knowledge of God (Eph. 1:17). Moreover, the Spirit operates within the Body of Christ, as we shall elaborate later.

b. *The unity of Scripture*

Because the Bible is the Word of God, it has a fundamental unity. This is a unity of origin, since he who has revealed himself does not contradict himself. It is also a unity of message and aim. For our Lord said the Scriptures 'bear witness to me' (Jn. 5:39; cf Lk. 24:25–27). Similarly, we read that 'the sacred writings . . . are able to instruct you for salvation through faith in Christ Jesus' (2 Tim. 3:15). Thus God's purpose through Scripture is to bear testimony to Christ as Saviour, to persuade all men and women to come to him for salvation, to lead them into maturity in Christ, and to send them into the world with the same good news.

In the midst of great diversity of content, therefore, Scripture has a single meaning, which permeates and illuminates all the partial meanings. We renounce every attempt to impose on Scripture an artificial unity, or even to insist on a single overarching concept. Instead, we discover in Scripture a God-given unity, which focuses on the Christ who died and rose again. for us and who offers to all his people his own new life, which is the same in every age and culture. This centrality of Christ in the Scriptures is a fundamental hermeneutical key.

c. *Biblical criticism*

Since the Bible is God's Word through human words, therefore under the guidance of the Holy Spirit, who is the only one who leads us into the understanding of Scripture, we must use scientific critical tools for its elucidation, and we appreciate the positive gains of modern biblical scholarship. Human criticism and the Spirit of God are not mutually exclusive. By 'criticism' we do not mean that we stand in judgment upon God's Word, but rather that we must investigate the historical, cultural and literary background of the biblical books.

We must also try to be aware of the presuppositions we bring to our study of the text. For none of us lives in a religion- or culture-free vacuum. What we must seek to ensure is that our presuppositions are Christian rather than secular. Some of the presuppositions of secular philosophy which have vitiated the critical study of the Bible are (a) evolutionary (that religion developed from below instead of being revealed from above), (b) anti-supernatural (that miracles cannot happen and that therefore the biblical miracles are legendary), and (c) demythologizing (that the thought world in which the biblical message was given is entirely incompatible with the modern age and must be discarded). Sociological presuppositions are equally dangerous, as when we read into Scripture the particular economic system we favour, whether capitalist or communist, or any other.

One test by which our critical methodology may be assessed is whether or not it enables people to hear the biblical message as good news of God revealing and giving himself in the historic death and resurrection of Christ.

d. The 'literal' sense

The first task of all critical study is to help us discover the original intention of the authors. What is the literary genre in which they wrote? What did they intend to say? What did they intend us to understand? For this is the 'literal' sense of Scripture, and the search for it is one of the most ancient principles which the Church affirmed. We must never divorce a text from its biblical or cultural context, but rather think ourselves back into the situation in which the word was first spoken and heard.

e. A contemporary message

To concentrate entirely on the ancient text, however, would lead us into an unpractical antiquarianism. We have to go beyond the original meaning to the contemporary message. Indeed, there is an urgent need for the Church to apply the teaching of Scripture creatively to the complex questions of today. Yet in seeking for relevance, we must not renounce faithfulness. The ancient and the modern, the original and the contemporary, always belong together. A text still means what its writer meant.

In this dialectic between the old and the new, we often become conscious of a clash of cultures, which calls for great spiritual sensitivity. On the one hand, we must be aware of the ancient cultural terms in which God spoke his word, so that we may discern between his eternal truth and its transient setting. On the other, we must be aware of the modern cultures and world views which condition us, some of whose values can make us blind and deaf to what God wants to say to us.

(iii) The Church's Teaching Authority

It is one thing to have a set of principles for biblical interpretation; it is another to know how to use them. How are these principles to be applied, and who is responsible for applying them?

a. The individual and the community

Evangelicals, who since the Reformation have emphasized both 'the priesthood of all believers' and 'the right of private judgment', insist on the duty and value of personal Bible study. The Second Vatican Council also urged that 'easy access to sacred Scripture should be provided for all the Christian faithful'.[13]

Both Evangelicals and Roman Catholics, however, recognize the dangers which arise from making Scripture available to all Christian people and from exhorting them to read it. How can they be protected from false interpretations? What safeguards can be found? Whether we are Evangelicals or Roman Catholics, our initial answer to these questions is the same: the major check to individualistic exegesis is the Holy Spirit who dwells and works in the Body of Christ, which is the Church. The Scriptures must be interpreted within the Christian community. It is only 'with all the saints' that we can comprehend the full dimensions of God's love (Eph. 3:18).

Roman Catholics also say that Scripture is interpreted by the Church. Yet the Church's task, paradoxically speaking, is at one and the same time to submit totally to the witness of Scripture in order to listen to God's Word, and to interpret it with authority. The act of authority in interpreting God's Word is an act of obedience to it.

But how in practice does the Christian community help us towards truth and restrain us from error? We are agreed that Christ has always intended his Church to have gifted and authorized teachers, both scholars and pastors. When Philip asked the Ethiopian whether he understood the Old Testament passage he was reading, he replied, 'How can I, unless some one guides me?' (Acts 8:31).

Many of our teachers belong to the past. Both Evangelicals and Roman Catholics have inherited a rich legacy of tradition. We cherish creeds, confessions and conciliar statements. We peruse the writings of the Fathers of the Church. We read books and commentaries.

Christ also gives his Church teachers in the present (Eph. 4:11), and it is the duty of Christian people to listen to them respectfully. The regular context for this is public worship in which the Word of God is read and expounded. In addition, we attend Church Synods and Councils, and national, regional and international conferences at which, after prayer and debate, our Christian understanding increases.

Respectful listening and mutual discussion are healthy; they are quite different from uncritical acquiescence. Both Evangelicals and Roman Catholics are troubled by the authoritarian influence which is being exerted by some strong, charismatic leaders and teachers of different backgrounds. The kind of thoughtless submission which is sometimes given to such was firmly discouraged by the apostles. The people of Beroea were commended because they examined the Scriptures to see whether Paul's preaching was true (Acts 17:11). Paul urged the Thessalonians to 'test everything', and John to 'test the spirits', i.e. teachers claiming inspiration (1 Thess. 5:21; 1 John 4:1). Moreover, the criterion by which the apostles exhorted the people to evaluate all teachers was the deposit of faith, the truths which they had heard 'from the beginning' (1 John 2:24; 2 John 9).

b. The regulation of Christian belief

We all agree that the fact of revelation brings with it the need for interpretation. We also agree that in the interpretative task both the believing community and the individual believer must have a share. Our emphasis on these varies, however, for the Evangelical fears lest God's Word be lost in church traditions, while the Roman Catholic fears it will be lost in a multiplicity of idiosyncratic interpretations.

This is why Roman Catholics emphasize the necessary role of the *magisterium*, although Evangelicals believe that in fact it has not delivered the Roman Catholic Church from a diversity of viewpoints, while admittedly helping to discern between them.

Evangelicals admit that in their case too some congregations, denominations and institutions have a kind of *magisterium*. For they elevate their particular creed or confession to this level, since they use it as their official interpretation of Scripture and for the exercise of discipline.

Both Roman Catholics and Evangelicals cherish certain creeds and confessions which summarize their beliefs. They also agree that new formulations of faith may be written and affirmed for our times. Other doctrinal statements may be either revised, or replaced by better statements, if this seems to be required by a clearer understanding of Scripture or for a clearer proclamation of the good news. All of us accept our responsibility to listen ever more attentively to what the Spirit through the Word is saying to the churches, so that we may grow in the knowledge of God, in the obedience of faith and in a more faithful and relevant witness.

What, then, Evangelicals have asked, is the status (and the authority for Roman Catholics) of the various kinds of statement made by those in a ministry of official teaching? In reply, Roman Catholics say that the function of the *magisterium* is to regulate the formulations of the faith, so that they remain true to the teaching of Scripture. They also draw a distinction. On the one hand, there are certain *privileged formulations*—e.g. a formal definition in council by the College of Bishops, of which the Pope is the presiding member, or a similar definition by the Pope himself, in special circumstances and subject to particular conditions to express the faith of the Church. It is conceded that such definitions do not necessarily succeed in conveying all aspects of the truth they seek to express, and while what they express remains valid, the way it is expressed may not have the same relevance for all times and situations. Nevertheless, for Roman Catholics they do give a certainty to faith. Such formulations are very few, but very important. On the other hand, statements made by those who have a special teaching role in the Roman Catholic Church have different levels of authority (e.g. papal encyclicals and other pronouncements, decisions of provincial synods or councils etc.). These require to be treated with respect, but do not call for assent in the same way as the first category.

We all believe that God will protect his Church, for he has promised to do so and has given us both his Scriptures and his Spirit; our disagreement is on the means and the degree of his protection.

Roman Catholics believe that it is the authoritative teaching of the Church which has the responsibility for oversight in the interpretation of Scripture, allowing a wide freedom of understanding, but excluding some interpretations as inadmissable because erroneous.

Evangelicals, on the other hand, believe that God uses the Christian community as a whole to guard its members from error and evil. Roman Catholics also believe in this *sensus fidelium*. For in the New Testament Church members are urged: 'let the word of Christ dwell in you richly, teach and admonish one another' (Col. 3:16). They are also exhorted to 'see to it' that their brothers and sisters stand firm in truth and righteousness.[14]

(iv) Can the Church be Reformed?

a. The need for reform
So far in this first section of our Report we have concentrated on the Church's responsibility to teach. Can it also learn? Can the Church which gives instruction receive it? More particularly, can Scripture exercise a reforming role in the Church? Is the Church itself under the Scripture it expounds?

These are questions which the Roman Catholic Church put to itself anew during the Second Vatican Council, and has continued to ask itself since. Evangelicals, however, to whom continuous reformation by the Word of God has always been a fundamental concern, wonder whether the reform to which the Roman Catholic Church consented at Vatican II was radical enough. Has it been more than an *aggiornamento* of ecclesiastical institutions and liturgical forms? Has it touched the Church's theological life or central structures? Has there been an inner repentance?

At the same time, Roman Catholics have always asked whether Evangelicals, in the discontinuity of the sixteenth century Reformation, have not lost something essential to the gospel and the Church.

Yet we all agree that the Church needs to be reformed, and that its reformation comes from God. The one truth is in God himself. He is the reformer by the power of his Spirit according to the Scriptures. In order to discern what he may be saying, Christian individuals and communities need each other. Individual believers must keep their eyes on the wider community of faith, and churches must be listening to the Spirit, who may bring them correction or insight through an individual believer.

b. Our response to God's Word

We agree on the objectivity of the truth which God has revealed. Yet it has to be subjectively received, indeed 'apprehended', if through it God is to do his reforming work. How then should our response to revelation be described?

We all acknowledge the difficulties we experience in receiving God's Word. For as it comes to us, it finds each of us in our own social context and culture. True, it creates a new community, but this community also has its cultural characteristics derived both from the wider society in which it lives and from its own history which has shaped its understanding of God's revelation. So we have to be on the alert, lest our response to the Word of God is distorted by our cultural conditioning.

One response will be intellectual. For God's revelation is a rational revelation, and the Holy Spirit is the Spirit of truth. So the Christian community is always concerned to understand and to formulate the faith, so that it may preserve truth and rebut error.

Response to God's truth can never be purely cognitive, however. Truth in the New Testament is to be 'done' as well as 'known', and so to find its place in the life and experience of individuals and churches. Paul called this full response 'the obedience of faith' (Rom. 1:5; 16:26). It is a commitment of the whole person.

Understanding, faith and obedience will in their turn lead to proclamation. For revelation by its very nature demands communication. The believing and obeying community must be a witnessing community. And as it faithfully proclaims what it understands, it will increasingly understand what it proclaims.

Thus reform is a continuous process, a work of the Spirit of God through the agency of the Word of God.

2
The Nature of Mission

2

The Nature of Mission

The very existence of the Evangelical-Roman Catholic Dialogue on Mission testifies to our common commitment to mission. One of the factors which led to its inauguration was the publication of the Lausanne Covenant (1974) and of *Evangelii Nuntiandi*, Pope Paul VI's apostolic exhortation 'Evangelization in the Modern World' (1975). These two documents supplied some evidence of a growing convergence in our understanding of mission. Not that Evangelicals or Roman Catholics regard either of these statements as exhaustive, but they consider them valuable summaries and teaching tools.

(i) The Basis of Mission

In response to the common criticism that we have no right to evangelize among all peoples, we together affirm the universality of God's purposes. God's creation of the world and of all humankind means that all should be subject to his lordship (Ps. 24:1–2; Eph. 3:8–11). The call of Abraham and of Israel had the wider purpose that all nations might see God's glory in his people and come to worship him. In the New Testament Jesus sends his disciples out in proclamatory witness, leading to the apostolic mission to all nations. In his Epistle to the Romans Paul teaches that, since all without distinction have sinned, so all without distinction are offered salvation, Gentiles as well as Jews (3:22f; 10:12).

We are agreed that mission arises from the self-giving life and love of the triune God himself and from his eternal purpose for the whole creation. Its goal is the God-centred Kingdom of the Father, exhibited through the building of the body of Christ, and cultivated in the fellowship of the Spirit. Because of Christ's first coming and the outpouring of the Holy Spirit, Christian mission has an eschatological dimension: it invites men and women to enter the Kingdom of God through Christ the Son by the work and regeneration of the Spirit.

We all agree that the arrival of the messianic Kingdom through Jesus Christ necessitates the announcement of the good news, the summons to repentance and faith, and the gathering together of the people of God. Sometimes Jesus clearly used 'the Kingdom of God' and 'salvation' as synonyms.[15] For to announce the arrival of the Kingdom of God is to proclaim its realization in the coming of Jesus Christ. And the Church witnesses to the Kingdom when it manifests the salvation it has received.

At the same time, long-standing tensions exist between Roman Catholics and Evangelicals. While both sides affirm that the pilgrim Church is missionary by its very nature, its missionary activity is differently understood.

Vatican II defines the Church for Roman Catholics as 'the sacrament of salvation', the sign and promise of redemption to each and every person without exception. For them, therefore, 'mission' includes not only evangelization but also the service of human need, and the building up and expression of fellowship in the Church. It is the mission of the Church to anticipate the Kingdom of God as liberation from the slavery of sin, from slavery to the Law and from death; by the preaching of the gospel, by the forgiveness of sins and by sharing in the Lord's

Supper.[16] But the Spirit of God is always at work throughout human history to bring about the liberating reign of God.

Evangelization is the proclamation (by word and example) of the good news to the nations. The good news is that God's actions in Jesus Christ are the climax of a divine revelation and relationship that has been available to everyone from the beginning. Roman Catholics assert that the whole of humanity is in a collective history which God makes to be a history of salvation. The *mystērion* of the gospel is the announcement by the Church to the world of this merging of the history of salvation with the history of the world.

Evangelicals generally, on the other hand, do not regard the history of salvation as coterminous with the history of the world, although some are struggling with this question. The Church is the beginning and anticipation of the new creation, the firstborn among his creatures. Though all in Adam die, not all are automatically in Christ. So life in Christ has to be received by grace with repentance through faith. With yearning Evangelicals plead for a response to the atoning work of Christ in his death and resurrection. But with sorrow they know that not all who are called are chosen. Judgment (both here and hereafter) is the divine reaction of God to sin and to the rejection of the good news. 'Rich young rulers' still walk away from the kingdom of grace. Evangelization is therefore the call to those outside to come as children of the Father into the fulness of eternal life in Christ by the Spirit, and into the joy of a loving community in the fellowship of the Church.

(ii) Authority and Initiative in Mission

Primary Christian obedience, we agree, is due to the Lord Jesus Christ and is expressed in both our individual and our common life under his authority. Roman Catholics and Evangelicals recognize that the tension between ecclesiastical authority and personal initiative, as also between the institutional and the charismatic, has appeared throughout biblical and Church history.

While for Roman Catholics hierarchical structures of teaching and pastoral authority are essential, the servant Church, as described by the Second Vatican Council, is called to express herself more fully in the exercise of apostolic 'collegiality' and 'subsidiarity' (the principle that ecclesial decisions are made at the lowest level of responsibility).

Evangelicals have traditionally emphasized the personal right of every believer to enjoy direct access to God and the Scriptures. There is also among them a growing realization of the importance of the Church as the Body of Christ, which tempers personal initiative through the restraint and direction of the fellowship.

This issue of authority has a bearing on mission. Are missionaries sent, or do they volunteer, or is it a case of both? What is the status of religious orders, mission boards or missionary societies, and para-church organizations? How do they relate to the churches or other ecclesial bodies? How can a preoccupation with jurisdiction (especially geographical) be reconciled with the needs of subcultures, especially in urban areas, which are often overlooked?

Although our traditions differ in the way we respond to these questions, we all wish to find answers which take account both of Church structures and of the liberty of the Spirit outside them.

(iii) Evangelization and Socio-political Responsibility

The controversy over the relationship between evangelization and socio-political responsibility is not confined to Roman Catholics and Evangelicals; it causes debate between and among all Christians.

We are agreed that 'mission' relates to every area of human need, both spiritual and social. Social responsibility is an integral part of evangelization; and the struggle for justice can be a manifestation of the Kingdom of God. Jesus both preached and healed, and sent his disciples out to do likewise. His predilection for those without power and without voice continues God's concern in the Old Testament for the widow, the orphan, the poor and the defenceless alien.

In particular we agree:

(a) that serving the spiritual, social and material needs of our fellow human beings together constitutes love of neighbour and therefore 'mission'.

(b) that an authentic proclamation of the good news must lead to a call for repentance, and that authentic repentance is a turning away from social as well as individual sins.

(c) that since each Christian community is involved in the reality of the world, it should lovingly identify with the struggle for justice as a suffering community.

(d) that in this struggle against evil in society, the Christian must be careful to use means which reflect the spirit of the gospel. The Church's responsibility in a situation of injustice will include repentance for any complicity in it, as well as intercessory prayer, practical service, and prophetic teaching which sets forth the standards of God and his Kingdom.

We recognize that some Roman Catholics and some Evangelicals find it difficult to subscribe to any inseparable unity between evangelization and the kind of socio-political involvement which is described above. There is also some tension concerning the allocation of responsibility for social service and action. Roman Catholics accept the legitimacy of involvement by the Church as a whole, as well as by groups and individuals. Among Evangelicals, however, there are differences between the Lutheran, Reformed and Anabaptist traditional understandings of Church and society. All would agree that Christian individuals and groups have social responsibilities; the division concerns what responsibility is assigned to the Church as a whole.

(iv) God's Work Outside the Christian Community

We have written about the Church and the Kingdom. We are agreed that the concept of the Church implies a limitation, for we talk about 'church members' which infers that there are 'nonmembers'. But how widely should we understand the Kingdom of God? We all agree that God works within the Christian community, for there he rules and dwells. But does he also work outside, and if so how?

This is a question of major missiological importance. All of us are concerned to avoid an interpretation of the universal saving will of God, which makes salvation automatic without the free response of the person.

At least four common convictions have emerged from our discussions. They concern the great doctrines of creation, revelation, salvation and judgment.

1. *Creation.* God has created all humankind, and by right of creation all humankind belongs to God. God also loves the whole human family and gives to them all 'life and breath and everything' (Acts 17:25).

2. *Revelation.* There are elements of truth in all religions. These truths are the fruit of a revelatory gift of God. Evangelicals often identify their source in terms of general revelation, common grace or the remnant image of God in humankind. Roman Catholics more frequently associate them with the work of the Logos, the true light, coming into the world and giving light to every man (John 1:9), and with the work of his Holy Spirit.

3. *Salvation.* There is only one Saviour and only one gospel. There is no other name but Christ's, through whom anyone may be saved (Acts 4:12). So all who receive salvation are saved by the free initiative of God through the grace of Christ.

4. *Judgment.* While the biblical concept of judgment refers to both reward and punishment, it is clear that those who remain in sin by resisting God's free grace (whether they are inside or outside the visible boundaries of the Church) provoke his judgment, which leads to eternal separation from him. The Church itself also stands under the judgment of God whenever it refuses or neglects to proclaim the gospel of salvation to those who have not heard Christ's name.

The sphere for missionary activity is described differently

within each tradition. Roman Catholics would expect God's mercy to be exercised effectively in benevolent action of his grace for the majority of humankind, unless they specifically reject his offer. Such a position gives them cause for confidence. Evangelicals consider that this view has no explicit biblical justification, and that it would tend to diminish the evangelistic zeal of the Church. Evangelicals are therefore less optimistic about the salvation of those who have no personal relationship to God through Jesus Christ.

We all affirm that the missionary enterprise is a participation in the mission of Jesus and the mission of his Church. The urgency to reach all those not yet claimed by his Lordship impels our mission.

Whether or not salvation is possible outside the Christian community, what is the motivation for mission work? We agree that the following strong incentives urgently impel Christians to the task of mission:

(a) to further the glory of God; the earth should be a mirror to reflect his glory.
(b) to proclaim the Lordship of Jesus Christ; all men and women are called to submit to his authority.
(c) to proclaim that Christ has struggled with Satan and dethroned him; in baptism and conversion we renounce Satan's rule and turn to Christ and righteousness.
(d) to proclaim that man does not live by bread alone; the gospel of salvation is the perfect gift of God's loving grace.
(e) to hasten the return of the Lord—the eschatological dimension. We look for the day of the Lord when the natural order will be completely redeemed, the whole earth will be filled with the knowledge of the Lord, and people from every nation, people, tribe and tongue will praise the triune God in perfection.

3

The Gospel of Salvation

3

The Gospel of Salvation

Roman Catholics and Evangelicals share a deep concern for the content of the good news we proclaim. We are anxious on the one hand to be faithful to the living core of the Christian faith, and on the other to communicate it in contemporary terms. How then shall we define the gospel?

(i) Human Need

Diagnosis must always precede prescription. So, although human need is not strictly part of the good news, it is an essential background to it. If the gospel is good news of salvation, this is because human beings are sinners who need to be saved.

In our description of the human condition, however, we emphasize the importance of beginning positively. We affirm that all men and women are made by God, for God and in the image of God, and that sin has defaced but not destroyed this purpose and this image (Gen. 9:6; Jas. 3:9). Therefore, as the creation of God, human beings have an intrinsic worth and dignity. Also, because of the light which lightens everybody, we all have within us an innate desire for God which nothing else can satisfy. As Christians, we must respect every human being who is seeking God, even when the search is expressed in ignorance (Acts 17:23).

Nevertheless original sin has intervened. We have noted Thomas Aquinas' description of original sin, namely 'the loss of original justice' (i.e. a right relationship with God) and such 'concupiscence' as constitutes a fundamental disorder in human nature and relationships; so that all our desires are inclined towards the making of decisions displeasing to God.

Evangelicals insist that original sin has distorted every part of human nature, so that it is permeated by self-centredness. Consequently, the Apostle Paul describes all people as 'enslaved', 'blind', 'dead' and 'under God's wrath', and therefore totally unable to save themselves.[17]

Roman Catholics also speak of original sin as an injury and disorder which has weakened—though not destroyed—human free will. Human beings have 'lifted themselves up against God and sought to attain their goal apart from him'.[18] As a result this has upset the relationship linking man to God and 'has broken the right order that should reign within himself as well as between himself and other men and all creatures'.[19] Hence human beings find themselves drawn to what is wrong and *of themselves* unable to overcome the assaults of evil successfully, 'so that everyone feels as though bound by chains'.[20]

Clearly there is some divergence between Roman Catholics and Evangelicals in the way we understand human sin and need, as well as in the language we use to express them. Roman Catholics think Evangelicals overstress the corruption of human beings by affirming their 'total depravity' (i.e. that every part of our humanness has been perverted by the Fall), while Evangelicals think Roman Catholics underestimate it and are therefore unwisely optimistic about the capacity, ability and desire of human beings to respond to the grace of God. Yet we agree that all are sinners, and that all stand in need of a radical salvation which includes deliverance from the power of evil, together with reconciliation to God and adoption into his family.

(ii) The Person of Jesus Christ

The radical salvation which human beings need has been achieved by Jesus Christ. Evangelicals and Roman Catholics are agreed about the centrality of Christ and of what God has done through him for salvation. 'The Father has sent his Son as the Saviour of the world' (1 John 4:14). But who was this Saviour Jesus?

Jesus of Nazareth was a man, who went about doing good, teaching with authority, proclaiming the Kingdom of God, and making friends with sinners to whom he offered pardon. He made himself known to his apostles, whom he had chosen and with whom he lived, as the Messiah (Christ) promised by the Scriptures. He claimed a unique filial relation to God, whom in prayer he called his Father ('Abba'). He thus knew himself to be the Son of God, and exhibited the power and authority of God over nature, human beings and demonic powers. He also spoke of himself as the Son of man. He fulfilled the perfect obedience of the Servant in going even to death on the cross. Then God raised him from the dead, confirming that he was from the beginning the Son he claimed to be (Ps. 2:7). Thus he was both 'descended from David according to the flesh' and 'designated Son of God in power according to the Spirit of holiness by his resurrection from the dead' (Rom. 1:3,4). This is why his apostles confessed him as Lord and Christ, Son of God, Saviour of humankind, sent by the Father, agent through whom God created all things, in whom we have been chosen from before the foundation of the world (Eph. 1:4), the Word made flesh.

The Incarnation of the Son was an objective event in history, in which the divine Word took upon himself our human nature. Within a single person were joined full divinity and full humanity. Although this understanding of him was not precisely formulated until the theological debates of the early centuries, we all agree that the Chalcedonian Definition faithfully expresses the truths to which the New Testament bears witness.

The purposes of the Incarnation were to reveal the Father to us, since otherwise our knowledge of God would have been deficient; to assume our nature in order to die for our sins and so accomplish our salvation, since he could redeem only what he had assumed; to establish a living communion between God and human beings, since only the Son of God made human could communicate to human beings the life of God; to supply the basis of the *imitatio*, since it is the incarnate Jesus we are to follow; to reaffirm the value and dignity of humanness, since God was not ashamed to take on himself our humanity; to provide in Jesus the firstfruits of the new humanity, since he is the 'first born among many brethren' (Rom. 8:29); and to effect the redemption of the cosmos in the end.

So then, in fidelity to the gospel and in accordance with the Scriptures, we together confess the person of Jesus Christ as the eternal Son of God, who was born of the Virgin Mary and became truly man, in order to be the Saviour of the world.

In our missionary task we have not only to confess Christ ourselves, but also to interpret him to others. As we do so, we have to consider, for example, how to reconcile for Jews and Moslems the monotheism of the Bible with the divine sonship of Jesus, how to present to Hindus and Buddhists the transcendent personality of God, and how to proclaim to adherents of traditional religion and of the new religious consciousness the supreme Lordship of Christ. Our Christology must always be both faithful to Scripture and sensitive to each particular context of evangelization.

(iii) The Work of Jesus Christ

It was this historic person, Jesus of Nazareth, fully God and fully human, through whom the Father acted for the redemption and reconciliation of the world. Indeed, only a person who was both God and human could have been the mediator between God and human beings. Because he was human he could represent us and identify with us in our weakness. Because he was God he could bear our sin and destroy the power of evil.

This work of redemption was accomplished supremely through the death of Jesus Christ, although we acknowledge the unity of his incarnate life, atoning death and bodily resurrection. For his death completed the service of his life (Mk. 10:45) and his resurrection confirmed the achievement of his death (Rom. 4:25).

Christ was without sin, and therefore had no need to die. He died for our sins, and in this sense 'in our place'. We are agreed about this basic truth and about other aspects of the Atonement. But in our discussion two different emphases have emerged, which we have summarized by the words 'substitution' and 'solidarity', although these concepts are not altogether exclusive.

Evangelicals lay much stress on the truth that Christ's death was 'substitutionary'. In his death he did something which he did not do during his life. He actually 'became sin' for us (2 Cor. 5:21) and 'became a curse' for us (Gal. 3:13). Thus God himself in Christ propitiated his own wrath, in order to avert it from us. In consequence, having taken our sin, he gives us his righteousness. We stand accepted by God in Christ, not because Christ offered the Father our obedience, but because he bore our sin and replaced it with his righteousness.

Roman Catholics express Christ's death more in terms of 'solidarity'. In their understanding Jesus Christ in his death made a perfect offering of love and obedience to his Father, which recapitulated his whole life. In consequence, we can enter into the sacrifice of Christ and offer ourselves to the Father in and with him. For he became one with us in order that we might become one with him.

Thus the word 'gospel' has come to have different meanings in our two communities.

For Evangelicals, it is the message of deliverance from sin, death and condemnation, and the promise of pardon, renewal and indwelling by Christ's Spirit. These blessings flow from Christ's substitutionary death. They are given by God solely through his grace, without respect to our merit, and are received solely through faith. When we are accepted by Christ, we are part of his people, since all his people are 'in' him.

For Roman Catholics the gospel centres in the person, message and gracious activity of Christ. His life, death and resurrection are the foundation of the Church, and the Church carries the living gospel to the world. The Church is a real sacrament of the gospel.

So the difference between us concerns the relationship between the gospel and the Church. In the one case, the gospel reconciles us to God through Christ and thus makes us a part of his people; in the other, the gospel is found within the life of his people, and thus we find reconciliation with God.

Although pastoral, missionary and cultural factors may lead us to stress one or other model of Christ's saving work, the full biblical range of words (e.g. victory, redemption, propitiation, justification, reconciliation) must be preserved, and none may be ignored.

The Resurrection, we agree, lies at the heart of the gospel and has many meanings. It takes the Incarnation to its glorious consummation, for it is the human Christ Jesus who reigns glorified at the Father's right hand, where he represents us and prays for us. The Resurrection was also the Father's vindication of Jesus, reversing the verdict of those who condemned and crucified him, visibly demonstrating his sonship, and giving us the assurance that his atoning sacrifice had been accepted. It is the resurrected and exalted Lord who sent his Spirit to his Church and who, claiming universal authority, now sends us into the world as his witnesses. The Resurrection was also the beginning of God's new creation, and is his pledge both of our resurrection and of the final regeneration of the universe.

(iv) The Uniqueness and Universality of Jesus Christ

In a world of increasing religious pluralism we affirm together the absolute uniqueness of Jesus Christ. He was unique in his person, in his death and in his resurrection. Since in no other person has God become human, died for the sins of the world and risen from death, we declare that he is the only way to God (Jn. 14:6), the only Saviour (Acts 4:12) and the only Mediator (1 Tim. 2:5). No one else has his qualifications.

The uniqueness of Jesus Christ implies his universality. The one and only is meant for all. We therefore proclaim him both 'the Saviour of the world' (Jn. 4:42) and 'Lord of all' (Acts 10:36).

We have not been able to agree, however, about the implications of his universal salvation and lordship. Together we believe that 'God . . . desires all men to be saved and to come to the knowledge of the truth' (1 Tim. 2:4), that the offer of salvation in Christ is extended to everybody, that the Church has an irreplaceable responsibility to announce the good news of salvation to all peoples, that all who hear the gospel have an obligation to respond to it, and that those who respond to it are incorporated into God's new, worldwide, multi-racial, multi-cultural community, which is the Father's family, the Body of Christ and the temple of the Holy Spirit. These aspects of the universality of Christ we gladly affirm together.

Roman Catholics go further, however, and consider that, if human sin is universal, all the more is Christ's salvation universal. If everyone born into the world stands in solidarity with the disobedience of the first Adam, still the human situation as such has been changed by the definitive event of salvation, that is, the Incarnation of the Word, his death, his resurrection and his gift of the Spirit. All are now part of the humanity whose new head has overcome sin and death. For all there is a new possibility of salvation which colours their entire situation, so that it is possible to say, 'Every person, without exception, has been redeemed by Christ, and with each person, without any exception, Christ is in some way united, even when that person is not aware of that'.[21] To become beneficiaries of the obedience of the Second Adam, men and women must turn to God and be born anew with Christ into the fulness of his life. The mission of the Church is to be the instrument to awaken this response by proclaiming the gospel, itself the gift of salvation for everyone who receives it, and to communicate the truth and grace of Christ to all.[22]

Evangelicals, on the other hand, understand the universality of Christ differently. He is universally present as God (since God is omnipresent) and as potential Saviour (since he offers salvation to all), but not as actual Saviour (since not all accept his offer). Evangelicals wish to preserve the distinction, which they believe to be apostolic, between those who are in Christ and those who are not (who consequently are in sin and under judgment), and so between the old and new communities. They insist on the reality of the transfer from one community to the other, which can be realized only through the new birth: 'if anyone is in Christ, he is a new creation' (2 Cor. 5:17).

The relationship between the life, death and resurrection of Jesus and the whole human race naturally leads Roman Catholics to ask whether there exists a possibility of salvation for those who belong to non-Christian religions and even for atheists. Vatican II was clear on this point: 'Those also can attain to everlasting salvation who through no fault of their own do not know the Gospel of Christ or his Church'. On the one hand, there are those who 'sincerely seek God and, moved by his grace, strive by their deeds to do his will'. On the other, there are those who 'have not yet arrived at an explicit knowledge of God, but who strive to live a good life, thanks to his grace'.[23] Both groups are prepared by God's grace to receive his salvation either when they hear the gospel or even if they do not. They can be saved by Christ, in a mysterious relation to his Church.

Evangelicals insist, however, that according to the New Testament those outside Christ are 'perishing', and that they can receive salvation only in and through Christ. They are therefore deeply exercised about the eternal destiny of those who have never heard of Christ. Most Evangelicals believe that, because they reject the light they have received, they condemn themselves to hell. Many are more reluctant to pronounce on their destiny, have no wish to limit the sovereignty of God, and prefer to leave this issue to him. Others go further in expressing their openness to the possibility that God may save some who have not heard of Christ, but immediately add that, if he does so, it will not be because of their religion, sincerity or actions (there is no possibility of salvation by good works), but only because of his own grace freely given on the ground of the atoning death of Christ. All Evangelicals recognize the urgent need to proclaim the gospel of salvation to all humankind. Like Paul in his message to the Gentile audience at Athens, they declare that God 'commands all men everywhere to repent, because he has fixed a day on which he will judge the world in righteousness by a man whom he has appointed' (Acts 17:30, 31).

(v) The Meaning of Salvation

In the Old Testament salvation meant rescue, healing and restoration for those already related to God within the covenant. In the New Testament it is directed to those who have not yet entered into the new covenant in Jesus Christ.

Salvation has to be understood in terms of both salvation history (the mighty acts of God through Jesus Christ) and salvation experience (a personal appropriation of what God has done through Christ). Roman Catholics and Evangelicals together strongly emphasize the objectivity of God's work through Christ, but Evangelicals tend to lay more emphasis than Roman Catholics on the necessity of a personal response to, and experience of, God's saving grace. To describe this, again the full New Testament vocabulary is needed (for example, the forgiveness of sins, reconciliation with God, adoption into his family, redemption, the new birth—all of which are gifts brought to us by the Holy Spirit), although Evangelicals still give paramount importance to justification by grace through faith.

We agree that what is offered us through the death and resurrection of Christ is essentially 'deliverance', viewed both negatively and positively. Negatively, it is a rescue from the power of Satan, sin and death, from guilt, alienation (estrangement from God), moral corruption, self-centredness, existential despair and fear of the future, including death. Positively, it is a deliverance into the freedom of Christ. This freedom brings human fulfilment. It is essentially becoming 'sons in the Son' and therefore brothers to each other. The unity of the disciples of Jesus is a sign both that the Father sent the Son and that the Kingdom has arrived. Further, the new community expresses itself in eucharistic worship, in serving the needy (especially the poor and disenfranchised), in open fellowship with people of every age, race and culture, and in conscious continuity with the historic Christ through fidelity to the teaching of his apostles. Is salvation broader than this? Does it include socio-political liberation?

Roman Catholics draw attention to the three dimensions of evangelization which *Evangelii Nuntiandi* links. They are the *anthropological*, in which humanity is seen always within a concrete situation; the *theological*, in which the unified plan of God is seen within both creation and redemption; and the *evangelical*, in which the exercise of charity (refusing to ignore human misery) is seen in the light of the story of the Good Samaritan.

We all agree that the essential meaning of Christ's salvation is the restoration of the broken relationship between sinful humanity and a saving God; it cannot therefore be seen as a temporal or material project, making evangelism unnecessary.

This restoration of humanity is a true 'liberation' from enslaving forces; yet this work has taken on an expanded and particular meaning in Latin America. Certainly God's plan of which Scripture speaks includes his reconciliation of human beings to himself and to one another.

The socio-political consequences of God's saving action through Christ have been manifest throughout history. They still are. Specific problems (e.g. slavery, urbanization, church-state relations, and popular religiosity) have to be seen both in their particular context and in relation to God's overall plan as revealed in Scripture and experienced in the believing community through the action of the Spirit.

Appendix: The Role of Mary in Salvation

Roman Catholics would rather consider the question of Mary in the context of the Church than of salvation. They think of her as a sinless woman, since she was both overshadowed by the Spirit at the Incarnation (Lk. 1:35) and baptized with the Spirit on the Day of Pentecost (Acts 1:14f and 2:1-4). She thus represents all Christians who have been made alive by the Spirit, and Roman Catholics speak of her as the 'figure' or 'model' of the Church.

The reason why we have retained this section on Mary within

the chapter on 'The Gospel of Salvation' (albeit as an Appendix) is that it is in the context of salvation that Evangelicals have the greatest difficulty with Marian teaching and that we discussed her role at ERCDOM II.

The place of Mary in the scheme of salvation has always been a sensitive issue between Roman Catholics and Evangelicals. We have tried to face it with integrity.

a. The interpretation of Scripture

It raises in an acute form the prior question how we use and interpret the Bible. We are agreed that biblical exegesis begins with a search for the 'literal' sense of a text, which is what its author meant. We further agree that some texts also have a 'spiritual' meaning, which is founded on the literal but goes beyond it because it was intended by the Divine—though not necessarily the human—author (e.g. Is. 7:14). This is often called the *sensus plenior*. The difference between Roman Catholics and Evangelicals lies in the degree to which the spiritual sense may be separated from the literal. Both sides agree that, whenever Scripture is not explicit, there is need for some check on the extravagances of interpreters. We are also agreed that this check is supplied by the context, both the immediate context and the whole of Scripture, which is a unity. Roman Catholics, however, say that Scripture must be read in the light of the living, developing tradition of the church, and that the Church has authority to indicate what the true meaning of Scripture is. Thus, in relation to Mary, Roman Catholics concede that devotion to Mary was a post-apostolic practice, but add that it was a legitimate development, whereas Evangelicals believe it has been unwarrantably imported into the Roman Catholic interpretation of Scripture.

b. Mary and Salvation

In one of our ERCDOM II sessions, entitled "The Place of the Virgin Mary in Salvation and Mission", and Evangelical response was made to Pope Paul VI's 1974 apostolic charge *Marialis Cultus* ('To Honour Mary'). Evangelical members of the dialogue asked for an explanation of two expressions in it which, at least on the

ERCR-D

The Library
INTERNATIONAL CHRISTIAN
GRADUATE UNIVERSITY

surface, appeared to them to ascribe to Mary an active and participatory role in the work of salvation.

The first (I.5) describes the Christmas season as a prolonged commemoration of Mary's 'divine, virginal and salvific Motherhood'. In what sense, Evangelicals asked, could Mary's motherhood be called 'salvific'? The Roman Catholics replied that the explanation of the term was to be found in the text itself, namely that she 'brought the Saviour into the world' by her obedient response to God's call.

The second passage (I.15) refers to 'the singular place' that belongs to Mary in Christian worship, not only as 'the holy Mother of God' but as 'the worthy Associate of the Redeemer'. In what sense, Evangelicals asked, could Mary properly be described as the Redeemer's 'worthy Associate'? It did not mean, the Roman Catholics responded, that she was personally without need of redemption, for on the contrary she was herself saved through her Son's death. In her case, however, 'salvation' did not signify the forgiveness of sins, but that, because of her predestination to be the 'Mother of God', she was preserved from original sin ('immaculate conception') and so from sinning. Positively, she could be described as the Redeemer's 'Associate' because of her unique link with him as his mother. The word should not give offence, for we too are 'associates of the Redeemer' both as recipients of his redemption and as agents through whose prayers, example, sacrifice, service, witness and suffering his redemption is proclaimed to others.

The Evangelicals made a double response to these explanations. First, they still found the language ambiguous, and considered this ambiguity particularly unfortunate in the central area of salvation. Secondly, they felt the whole Roman Catholic emphasis on Mary's role in salvation exaggerated, for when the apostles John and Paul unfold the mystery of the Incarnation, it is to honour Christ the Son not Mary the mother. At the same time, they readily agreed that in Luke's infancy narrative Mary is given the unique privilege of being the Saviour's mother, and on that account is addressed as both 'highly favoured' and 'blessed among women' (1:28, 42). If Evangelicals are to be true to their stance on *sola Scriptura*, they must therefore overcome any inhibitions they may have and faithfully expound such texts.

Our discussion also focused on the use of the term 'co-operation'. For example, it is stated in *Lumen Gentium* chapter VIII that Mary is rightly seen as 'co-operating in the work of human salvation through free faith and obedience' (II, 56), and again that 'the unique mediation of the Redeemer does not exclude but rather gives rise . . . to a manifold co-operation which is but a sharing in this unique source' (III, 62). The Evangelicals agreed that the notion of co-operation with God is biblical (e.g. 'workers together with him' (2 Cor. 6:1)), but pointed out that this refers to a divine-human partnership in which our share lies in the *proclaiming*, and not in any sense in the *procuring*, of salvation. The Roman Catholics agreed. The 'co-operation' between Christ and us, they said, does not mean that we can add anything to Christ or his work, since he is complete in himself, and his work has been achieved. It means rather that we share in the benefits of what he has done (not in the doing of it) and that (by his gift alone, as in the case of Mary) we offer ourselves to him in gratitude, to spend our lives in his service, and to be used by him as instruments of his grace (vid. Gal. 1). The Evangelicals were relieved, but still felt that the use of the word 'co-operation' in this sense was inappropriate.

Another word we considered was 'mediatrix', the feminine form of 'mediator'. The Evangelicals reacted with understandable vehemence against its application to Mary, as did also some Roman Catholics. She must not be designated thus, they insisted, since the work of mediation belongs to Christ alone. In reply, the Roman Catholics were reassuring. Although the word (or rather its Greek equivalent) was used of Mary from the fifth century onwards, and although some bishops were pressing at Vatican II for its inclusion in the text, the Council deliberately avoided it. It occurs only once, and then only in a list of Mary's traditional titles. Moreover, in the same section of *Lumen Gentium* (III, 60–62) Christ is twice called 'the one Mediator' in accordance with 1 Timothy 2:5–6, and his 'unique mediation' is also referred to twice, which (it is added) Mary's maternal ministry 'in no way obscures or diminishes'.

The Final Document deriving from the Puebla Conference on

the Evangelization of Latin America (1979), which contains a long section entitled 'Mary, Mother and Model of the Church' (paras. 282–303), was cited by Evangelical participants. Paragraph 293 declares that Mary 'now lives immersed in the mystery of the Trinity, praising the glory of God and interceding for human beings'. Evangelicals find this a disturbing expression, and not all Roman Catholics are happy with it, finding it too ambiguous (if indeed 'immersed' is an accurate translation of the Spanish original *inmersa:* there has been some controversy about this). Roman Catholics explain that the notion of Mary's 'immersion' in the Trinity means that she is the daughter of the Father, the mother of the Son, and the temple of the Holy Spirit (all three expressions being used in paragraph 53 of *Lumen Gentium*). But in addition they point out that neither the Puebla document nor popular expressions of Marian piety are normative for Roman Catholic belief about Mary which is to be found rather in chapter 8 of *Lumen Gentium,* Vatican II's "Dogmatic Constitution on the Church".

The fears of Evangelicals were to some extent allayed by these Roman Catholic explanations and assurances. Yet a certain Evangelical uneasiness remained. First, the traditional Catholic emphasis on Mary's role in salvation (e.g. as the 'New Eve', the life-giving mother) still seemed to them incompatible with the much more modest place accorded to her in the New Testament. Secondly, the vocabulary used in relation to Mary seemed to them certainly ambiguous and probably misleading. Is it not vitally important, they asked, especially in the central doctrine of salvation through Christ alone, to avoid expressions which require elaborate explanation (however much hallowed by long tradition) and to confine ourselves to language which is plainly and unequivocally Christ-centred?

At the same time Roman Catholics are troubled by what seems to them a notable neglect by Evangelicals of the place given by God to Mary in salvation history and in the life of the Church.

4

Our Response in the Holy Spirit to the Gospel

4

Our Response in the Holy Spirit
to the Gospel

We agree that evangelism is not just a proclamation of Christ's historic work and saving offer. Evangelism also includes a call for response which is often called 'conversion'.

(i) The Work of the Holy Spirit

This response, however, does not depend on the efforts of the human person, but on the initiative of the Holy Spirit. As is stated in the Scripture, 'for by grace you have been saved through faith; and this is not your own doing, it is the gift of God —not because of works, lest any man should boast' (Eph. 2:8–9). There is therefore a trinitarian dimension to the human person's response: it is the Father who gives; his supreme gift is his Son, Jesus Christ for the life of the world (Jn. 6:23); and it is the Holy Spirit who opens our minds and hearts so that we can accept and proclaim that Jesus Christ is Lord (1 Cor. 12:3) and live as his disciples. This means that the Holy Spirit guarantees that the

55

salvation which the Father began in Jesus Christ becomes effective in us in a personal way.

When human persons experience conversion, the Holy Spirit illumines their understanding so that Jesus Christ can be confessed as the Truth itself revealed by the Father (Jn. 14:6). The Holy Spirit also renders converted persons new creatures, who participate in the eternal life of the Father and the Son (Jn. 11:25–26). Furthermore, the Holy Spirit, through the gifts of faith, hope and love, already enables converted persons to have a foretaste of the Kingdom which will be totally realized when the Son hands over all things to the Father (1 Cor. 15:28).

Thus, the work of the Holy Spirit in Christian conversion has to be seen as the actual continuation of his previous creative and redemptive activity throughout history. Indeed, at the beginning the Holy Spirit was present at the act of creation (Gen. 1:2), and he is continually sent forth as the divine breath by whom everything is created and by whom the face of the earth is renewed (Ps. 104:29–30). Although all persons are influenced by the life-giving Spirit of God, it is particularly in the Old Testament, which he inspired, that the recreative work of the Holy Spirit, after the fall of humankind, is concretely manifested. In order to ground the divine plan to recreate humanity, the Holy Spirit first taught the patriarchs to fear God and to practise righteousness. And to assemble his people Israel and to bring it back to the observance of the Covenant, the Holy Spirit raised up judges, kings and wise men. Moreover, the prophets, under the guidance of the Spirit, announced that the Holy Spirit would create a new heart and bestow new life by being poured out in a unique way on Israel and, through it, on all humanity (Ezek. 36:24–28; Joel 2:28–29).

The recreative work of the Holy Spirit reached its culminating point in the incarnation of Jesus Christ who, as the New Adam, was filled with the Holy Spirit without measure (Jn. 3:34). Because Jesus Christ was the privileged bearer of the Holy Spirit, he is the one who gives the Holy Spirit for the regeneration of human beings: 'He on whom you see the Spirit descend and remain, this is he who baptizes with the Holy Spirit' (Jn. 1:33). Through his death on behalf of sinful humankind and his rising up to glory, Jesus Christ communicates the Holy Spirit to all who are converted to him, that is, receive him by faith as their personal Lord and Saviour. This new life in Jesus Christ by the Holy Spirit is signified by baptism and by membership in the Body of Christ, the Church. Furthermore, through his indwelling in converted persons, the Holy Spirit attests that they are co-heirs with Christ of eternal glory.

(ii) Conversion and Baptism

We have been agreeably surprised to discover a considerable consensus among us that repentance and faith, conversion and baptism, regeneration and incorporation into the Christian community all belong together, although we have needed to debate their relative positions in the scheme of salvation.

'Conversion' signifies an initial turning to Jesus Christ in repentance and faith, with a view to receiving the forgiveness of sins and the gift of the Spirit, and to being incorporated into the Church, all signed to us in baptism (Acts 2:38, 39). The expression 'continuous conversion' (if used) must therefore be understood as referring to our daily repentance as Christians, our response to new divine challenges, and our gradual transformation into the image of Christ by the Spirit (2 Cor. 3:18). Moreover, some who have grown up in a Christian home find themselves to be regenerate Christians without any memory of a conscious conversion.

We agree that baptism must never be isolated, either in theology or in practice, from the context of conversion. It belongs essentially to the whole process of repentance, faith, regeneration by the Holy Spirit, and membership of the covenant community, the Church. A large number of Evangelicals (perhaps the majority) practise only 'believers' baptism'. That is, they baptise only those who have personally accepted Jesus Christ as their Saviour and Lord, and they regard baptism both as the convert's public profession of faith and as the dramatization (by immersion in water) of his or her having died and risen with Christ. The practice of infant baptism (practised by some

Evangelicals, rejected by others) assumes both that the parents believe and will bring their children up in the Christian faith, and that the children will themselves later come to conscious repentance and faith.

We rejoice together that the whole process of salvation is the work of God by the Holy Spirit. And it is in this connection that Roman Catholics understand the expression *ex opere operato* in relation to baptism. It does not mean that the sacraments have a mechanical or automatic efficacy. Its purpose rather is to emphasize that salvation is a sovereign work of *Christ,* in distinction to a Pelagian or semi-Pelagian confidence in human ability.

There is a further dimension of the work of the Holy Spirit in our response to the gospel to which we have become increasingly sensitive, and which we believe belongs within our understanding of the work of the Spirit in mission.

In the light of biblical teaching, particularly in the Epistle to the Ephesians,[24] and also in view of the insights gained through Christian missionary experience, we believe that, although the revelation of Jesus Christ as the Truth by the Holy Spirit is in itself complete in the Scriptures, nevertheless he is wanting to lead the Church into a yet fuller understanding of this revelation. Hence we rejoice that in the various cultural contexts in which men and women throughout nearly twenty centuries of Christian history have been enabled by the Holy Spirit to respond to the gospel, we can perceive the many-sidedness of the unique Lord Jesus Christ, the Saviour of all humankind.

Accordingly, we hope that the Holy Spirit will make us open to such new and further insights into the meaning of Jesus Christ, as he may wish to communicate by means of various manifestations of Christian life in our Christian communities, as well as in human societies where we earnestly desire that he will create a response to the gospel in conversion, baptism and incorporation into Christ's body, the Church.

(iii) Church Membership

Conversion and baptism are the gateway into the new community of God, although Evangelicals distinguish between the visible and invisible aspects of this community. They see conversion as the means of entry into the invisible church and baptism as the consequently appropriate means of entry into the visible church. Both sides agree that the church should be characterized by learning, worship, fellowship, holiness, service and evangelism (Acts 2:42–47). Furthermore, life in the Church is characterized by hope and love, as a result of the outpouring of the Holy Spirit: 'And hope does not disappoint us, because God's love has been poured into our hearts through the Holy Spirit which has been given to us' (Rom. 5:5). It is the Holy Spirit who arouses and sustains our response to the living Christ. Through the power of the Holy Spirit, the unity of the human family, which was disrupted by sin, is gradually being recreated as the new humanity emerges (Eph. 2:15).

The issue of church membership has raised in our dialogue the delicate and difficult question of the conversion of those already baptized. How are we to think of their baptism? And which church should they join? This practical question can cause grave problems in the relationship between Roman Catholics and Evangelicals. It is particularly acute in places like Latin America, where large numbers of baptized Roman Catholics have had a minimal relationship with the Roman Catholic Church since their baptism.

When such Roman Catholics have a conversion experience, many Evangelical churches welcome them into membership without re-baptizing them. Some Baptist churches, however, and some others, would insist on baptizing such converts, as indeed they baptize Protestant converts who have been baptized in infancy.

Then there is the opposite problem of Protestant Christians wishing to become members of the Roman Catholic Church. Since Vatican II the Roman Catholic Church has recognized other Christians as being in the first place 'brethren', rather than subjects for conversion. Nevertheless, since the Roman Catholic Church believes that the one Church of Christ subsists within it in a unique way, it further believes it is legitimate to receive other Christians into its membership. Such membership is not seen as an initial step towards salvation, however, but as a further step towards Christian growth. Considerable care is taken nowadays to ensure that such a step is not taken under wrong pressure and for unworthy motives. In other words, there is an avoidance of 'proselytism' in the wrong sense. Then, provided that there is some proof of valid baptism having taken place, there is no question of rebaptism.

Church members need constantly to be strengthened by the grace of God. Roman Catholics and Evangelicals understand grace somewhat differently, however, Roman Catholics thinking of it more as divine life and Evangelicals as divine favour. Both sides agree that it is by a totally free gift of the Father that we become joined to Christ and enabled to live like Christ through the power of the Holy Spirit. Both sides also understand the Eucharist (or Lord's Supper) as a sacrament (or ordinance) of grace. Roman Catholics affirm the real presence of the body and blood of Jesus Christ and emphasize the mystery of Christ and his salvation becoming present and effective by the working of the Holy Spirit under the sacramental sign,[25] whereas Evangelicals (in different ways according to their different Church traditions) view the sacrament as the means by which Christ blesses us by drawing us into fellowship with himself, as we remember his death until he comes again (1 Cor. 11:26).

Despite the lack of full accord which we have just described, both Evangelicals and Roman Catholics agree that the Eucharist is spiritual food and spiritual drink (1 Cor. 10:3–4, 16), because the unifying Spirit is at work in this sacrament. As a memorial of the New Covenant, the Eucharist is a privileged sign in which Christ's saving grace is especially signified and/or made available to Christians. In the Eucharist the Holy Spirit makes the words Jesus spoke at the Last Supper effective in the Church and assures Christians that through their faith they are intimately united to Christ and to each other in the breaking of the bread and the sharing of the cup.

(iv) Assurance of Salvation

It has always been traditional among Evangelicals to stress not only salvation as a present gift, but also the assurance of salvation enjoyed by those who have received it. They like, for example, to quote 1 Jn. 5:13: 'I write this to you who believe in the name of the Son of God, that you may know that you have eternal life'. Thus, eternal life begins in us now through the Spirit of the risen Christ, because we are 'raised with him through faith in the working of God, who raised him from the dead' (Col. 2:12). Yet in daily life we live in the tension between what is already given and what is still awaited as a promise, for 'your life is hid with Christ in God. When Christ who is our life appears, then you will also appear with him in glory' (Col. 3:3, 4).

Roman Catholics and Evangelicals are agreed that the only ground for assurance is the objective work of Christ; this ground does not lie in any way in the believer.

We speak somewhat differently about the work of Christ, however, and relate it differently in terms of practical piety. Evangelicals refer to the 'finished' work of Christ on the cross and rest their confidence wholly upon it. Roman Catholics also speak of Christ's work as having been done 'once for all'; they therefore see it as beyond repetition. Nevertheless, they understand that through the Eucharist Christ's unique, once-for-all work is made present, and that by this means they maintain a present relationship to it. The relationship to Christ's finished work which Evangelicals enjoy is maintained by faith, but it is faith in what was done, and what was done is never re-presented.

Roman Catholics and Evangelicals both claim an authentic religious experience, which includes an awareness of the presence of God and a taste for spiritual realities. Yet Evangelicals think Roman Catholics sometimes lack a visible joy in Christ, which their assurance has given them, whereas Roman Catholics think Evangelicals are sometimes insufficiently attentive to the New Testament warnings against presumption. Roman Catholics also claim to be more realistic than Evangelicals about the vagaries of religious experience. The actual experience of Evangelicals seldom leads them to doubt their salvation, but Roman Catholics know that the soul may have its dark nights. In summary, Evangelicals appear to Roman Catholics more pessimistic about human nature before conversion, but more optimistic about it afterwards, while Evangelicals allege the opposite about Roman Catholics. Roman Catholics and Evangelicals together agree that Christian assurance is more an assurance of faith (Heb. 10:22) than of experience, and that perseverance to the end is a gratuitous gift of God.

5

The Church and the Gospel

5

The Church and the Gospel

Evangelicals, because of their emphasis on the value of the individual, have traditionally neglected the doctrine of the Church. The topic was not neglected in our dialogue, however. We found ourselves united in certain convictions about the Church, and in our commitment to it. We were able to agree on a four-fold relationship between the Church and the gospel.

(i) The Church is a Part of the Gospel

The redemptive purpose of God has been from the beginning to call out a people for himself. When he called Abraham, he promised to bless all nations through his posterity, and has kept his promise. For all those who are united to Christ, Gentiles as well as Jews, arc Abraham's spiritual children and share in the promised blessing.[26]

This wonderful new thing, namely the abolition of the dividing wall between Jews and Gentiles and the creation of a single new humanity, was at the heart of Paul's gospel (Eph. 2:14, 15).

He called it 'the mystery of Christ' which, having been made known to him, he must make known to others (Eph. 3:3–9).

Both Evangelicals and Roman Catholics are conscious of past failure in their understanding of the Church. Roman Catholics used to concentrate on the Church as a hierarchical institution, but now (since Vatican II) see it in new perspective by stressing the important biblical images such as that of the People of God. Evangelicals have sometimes preached an excessively individualistic gospel, 'Christ died for me'. This is true (Gal. 2:20), but it is far from the whole truth, which is that Christ gave himself for us 'to purify for himself a people . . .' (Tit. 2:14).

Thus both Roman Catholics and Evangelicals agree that the Church as the Body of Christ is part of the gospel. That is to say, the good news includes God's purpose to create for himself through Christ a new, redeemed, united and international people of his own.

(ii) The Church is a Fruit of the Gospel

The first clear proclamation of the good news in the power of the Holy Spirit resulted in the gathered community of God's people—the Church (Acts 2:39–42). This was to become the pattern for subsequent apostolic and missionary endeavours with the gospel. The condition for membership of the community is *repentance* (chiefly from the sin of unbelief and rejection of Christ), and *faith* in the Lord Jesus Christ, witnessed to in submission to baptism in his name (Acts 2:38). The benefits of membership include the personal enjoyment of the forgiveness of sins, and participation in the new life of the Spirit (Acts 2:38, 39; 1 Cor. 12:13).

From the beginning, the community of God's people was marked by a devotion to the apostolic teaching, to fellowship (a sharing which extended to practical loving care), to the breaking of bread (the Lord's Supper), and to the prayers or public worship (Acts 2:42). To this *believing, worshipping, caring and witnessing* community, 'the Lord added to their number day by day those who were being saved' (Acts 2:47).

Evangelicals on the whole have tended to emphasize personal salvation almost to the point of losing sight of the central place of the Church. The multiplication of evangelistic organizations and agencies which are not church-based has contributed to this distortion. There is however a growing desire to correct it. For wherever the gospel goes, it bears fruit in the spread and growth of the Church.

(iii) The Church is an Embodiment of the Gospel

The very life of the Church as God's new community becomes itself a witness to the gospel. 'The life of the community only acquires its full meaning when it becomes a witness, when it evokes admiration and conversion and when it becomes the preaching and proclamation of the Good News'.[27] Thus the Church is the sign of the power and the presence of Jesus, the light of Christ shining out visibly to bring all men to that light.[28]

As a fellowship of communities throughout the world the Church is to be 'a people brought into unity from the unity of the Father, Son and Holy Spirit' (Cyprian). This was why Jesus had come into the world, and why the living communion of believers between themselves and the Lord of life, and between each other, is to be the proclamation that will move people's hearts to belief (Jn. 13:34, 35; 17:23).

In every place the believing community speaks to the world by an authentically Christian life given over to God in a communion that nothing shall destroy and at the same time given to one's neighbour with limitless zeal (cf. 1 Pet. 2:12).

It is also the community of peace which makes Jew and Gentile one, in which by the power of the broken body of Christ the enmity which stood like a dividing wall between them has been broken down and a single new humanity brought into being (Eph. 2:15–16). The Church cannot with integrity preach the gospel of reconciliation unless it is evidently a reconciled community itself.

It is a community that makes present the obedient Lord who underwent death for us. It is founded upon him (Eph. 2:20), he is its Lord (Eph. 1:22), and its power to speak of him comes from the manner in which it reproduces in all its members and in its common life his obedience to the saving plan of God.

This unity, holiness, love and obedience are the authentic sign that Christ is not an anonymous or remote Lord. They are the mark of the community given over to God, and they speak about the good news of salvation in Jesus Christ.

(iv) The Church is an Agent of the Gospel

That the Church must be an agent of the gospel overflows from its internal life. The Church which receives the Word must also sound it forth (1 Thes. 1:5–8). The Church which embodies its message visually must also declare it verbally.

First, the Church continues and prolongs the very same mission of Christ.[29]

Secondly, the Church received Christ's command to be his witnesses in the power of the Spirit to the ends of the earth (Acts 1:8).

Thirdly, the Church proclaims the message with the authority of the Lord himself, who gave her the power of the Spirit. As to the qualified subjects of this authority, there are divergences between Evangelicals and Roman Catholics. For Evangelicals the agent of the proclamation is the whole community of believers, who are equipped for this task by those appointed to the pastoral ministry (Eph. 4:11, 12). For Roman Catholics also the evangelistic task belongs to the whole people of God, but they believe bishops have a special role and responsibility both to order the life of the community for this task and, as successors to the ministry of apostolic times, to preach the good news of the Kingdom.

To sum up, the Church and the gospel belong indissolubly together. We cannot think of either apart from the other. For God's purpose to create a new community through Christ is itself an important element in the good news. The Church is also both the fruit and the agent of the gospel, since it is through the gospel that the Church spreads and through the Church that the gospel spreads. Above all, unless the Church embodies the gospel, giving it visible flesh and blood, the gospel lacks credibility and the Church lacks effectiveness in witness.

More and more Christians are recognizing this lack of a fully credible, effective witness because of divisions among themselves. They believe that Christ has called all his disciples in every age to be witnesses to him and his gospel to the ends of the earth (cf. Acts 1:8). Yet those who profess such discipleship differ about the meaning of the one gospel and go their different ways as if Christ himself were divided (cf. 1 Cor. 1:13).

To be sure, Christian separations and divisions have often been due to conscientiously held convictions, and Christian unity must not be sought at the expense of Christian truth. Nevertheless, the divisions and their causes contradict the will of Jesus Christ, who desires his people to be united in truth and love. They also hinder the proclamation of his good news of reconciliation. Therefore the gospel calls the Church to be renewed in truth, holiness and unity, in order that it may be effectively renewed for mission as well.

6
The Gospel and Culture

6

The Gospel and Culture

The influence of culture on evangelism, conversion and church formation is increasingly recognized as a topic of major missiological importance. The Willowbank Report *Gospel and Culture* (1978) defines culture as 'an integrated system of beliefs (about God or reality or ultimate meaning), of values (about what is true, good, beautiful and normative), of customs (how to behave, relate to others, talk, pray, dress, work, play, trade, farm, eat, etc.), and of institutions which express these beliefs, values and customs (government, law courts, temples or churches, family, schools, hospitals, factories, shops, unions, clubs, etc.), which binds a society together and gives it a sense of identity, dignity, security and continuity'.[30] Viewed thus, culture pervades the whole of human life, and it is essential for Christians to know how to evaluate it.

It is acknowledged that Evangelicals and Roman Catholics start from a different background. Evangelicals tend to stress the discontinuity, and Roman Catholics the continuity, between man unredeemed and man redeemed. At the same time, both emphases are qualified. Discontinuity is qualified by the Evangelical recognition of the image of God in humankind, and continuity by the Roman Catholic recognition that human beings and societies are contaminated by sin. The Lausanne Covenant summarized this tension as follows: 'Because man is God's creature, some of his culture is rich in beauty and goodness. Because he is fallen, all of it is tainted with sin and some of it is demonic'.[31]

We have particularly concentrated on the place of culture in four areas,—in the Bible, in cross-cultural evangelism, in conversion and in church formation.

(i) Culture and the Bible

We have already affirmed that the Bible is the Word of God through the words of human beings. Realizing that human language and human thought forms reflect human cultures, we saw the need to explore two major questions:

(a) what was the attitude of the biblical authors to their cultures?

(b) how should we ourselves react to the cultural conditioning of Scripture?

In answer to the first question, we considered the New Testament. Its message comes to us from the context of the first century world, with its own images and vocabulary, and is thus set in the context of that world's culture. The culture has become the vehicle of the message.

Yet within that first century culture there were elements which the Christian and the Church were required to resist, out of loyalty to the Lord Jesus. Distinctions between the new community and the surrounding culture were clearly drawn. At the same time, the Christian and the Church enjoyed a new freedom in Christ which enabled them to discern those elements in the culture which must be rejected as hostile to their faith and those which were compatible with it and could on that account be affirmed. Blindness, which leads Christians to tolerate the evil and/or overlook the good in their culture, is a permanent temptation.

Our other question was concerned with how we ourselves should react to the cultural conditioning of Scripture. It breaks down into two subsidiary questions which express the options before us. First, are the biblical formulations (which we have already affirmed to be normative) so intrinsically conditioned by their mode of specific cultural expression that they cannot be changed to suit different cultural settings? Put another way, has biblical inspiration (which Evangelicals and Roman Catholics both acknowledge) made the cultural forms themselves normative? The alternative is to ask whether it is the revealed teaching which is normative, so that this may be re-expressed in other cultural forms. We believe the latter to be the case, and that such re-expression or translation is a responsibility laid both on cross-cultural missionaries and on local Christian leaders.

(ii) Culture and Evangelization

Christian missionaries find themselves in a challenging cross-cultural, indeed tri-cultural, situation. They come from a particular culture themselves, they travel to people nurtured in another, and they take with them a biblical gospel which was originally formulated in a third. How will this interplay of cultures affect their evangelism? And how can they be simultaneously faithful to Scripture and relevant to the local culture?

In the history of mission in this century a progress is discernible. The successive approaches may be summarized as follows:

(a)   In the first period the missionary brought along with the gospel message many of the cultural trappings of his or her own situation. Then culture, instead of being (as in the New Testament) a vehicle for the proclamation of the gospel, became a barrier to it. Accidentals of teaching and practice were taught as if they were essentials, and a culture—Christianity was preached, as if it were the gospel.

(b) In the second period the gospel message was translated into terms (language and thought forms, artistic symbols and music) appropriate to those to whom it was brought, and the cultural trappings began to be left behind. Now local cultures, instead of being neglected, were respected and where possible used for the better communication of the gospel. In a word, the gospel began to be 'contextualized'.

(c) So at the present time, missionaries endeavour to bring both the biblical gospel and an experience of life in Christ. They also endeavour to take seriously the people to whom they have come, with their worldview and way of life, so that they may find their own authentic way of experiencing and expressing the salvation of Christ. This kind of evangelism tries to be both faithful to the biblical revelation and relevant to the people's culture. In fact, it aims at bringing Scripture, context and experience into a working relationship for the effective presentation of the gospel.

(iii) Culture and Conversion

We are clear that conversion includes repentance, and that repentance is a turning away from the old life. But what are the aspects of the old life from which a convert must turn away? Conversion cannot be just turning away from 'sin' as this is viewed in any one particular culture. For different cultures have different understandings of sin, and we have to recognize this aspect of pluralism. So missionaries and church leaders in each place need great wisdom, both at the time of a person's conversion and during his or her maturing as a Christian, to distinguish between the moral and the cultural, between what is clearly approved or condemned by the gospel on the one hand and by custom or convention on the other. The repentance of conversion should be a turning away only from what the gospel condemns.

(iv) Culture and Church Formation

In the development of the Christian Community in each place, as in the other areas we have mentioned, missionaries must avoid all cultural imperialism; that is, the imposition on the Church of alien cultural forms. Just as the gospel has to be inculturated, so must the Church be inculturated also.

We all agree that the aim of 'indigenization' or 'inculturation' is to make local Christians congenial members of the body of Christ. They must not imagine that to become Christian is to become western and so to repudiate their own cultural and national inheritance. The same principle applies in the west, where too often to become Christian has also meant to become middle class.

There are a number of spheres in which each Church should be allowed to develop its own identity. The first is the question of certain forms of organization, especially as they relate to Church leadership. Although Roman Catholics and Evangelicals take a different approach to authority and its exercise, we are agreed that in every Christian community (especially a new one) authority must be exercised in a spirit of service. 'I am among you as one who serves', Jesus said (Lk. 22:27). Yet the expression given to leadership can vary according to different cultures.

The second sphere is that of artistic creativity—for example church architecture, painting, symbols, music and drama. Local churches will want to express their Christian identity in artistic forms which reflect their local culture.

A third area is theology. Every church should encourage theological reflection on the aspirations of its culture, and seek to develop a theology which gives expression to these. Yet only in such a way as to apply, not compromise, the biblical revelation.

Two problems confront a church which is seeking to 'inculturate' itself, namely provincialism and syncretism. 'Provincialism' asserts the local culture of a particular church to the extent that it cuts itself adrift from, and even repudiates, other churches. We are agreed that new expressions of local church life must in no way break fellowship with the wider Christian community.

'Syncretism' is the attempt to fuse the biblical gospel with elements of local culture which, being erroneous or evil, are incompatible with it. But the gospel's true relation to culture is discriminating, judging some elements and welcoming others. The criteria it applies to different elements or forms include the questions whether they are under the judgment of Christ's lordship, and whether they manifest the fruit of the Spirit.

It has to be admitted that every expression of Christian truth is inadequate and may be distorted. Hence the need for mutually respectful dialogue about the relative merits of old and new forms, in the light of both the biblical revelation and the experience of the wider community of faith.

The Second Vatican Council addressed itself to these important matters. It recognized that in every culture there are some elements which may need to be 'purged of evil association' and to be restored 'to Christ their source, who overthrows the rule of the devil and limits the manifold malice of evil'. In this way 'the good found in people's minds and hearts, or in particular customs and cultures, is purified, raised to a higher level and reaches its perfection . . . .'.[32]

Hence it is not a question of adapting things which come from the world usurped by Satan, but of re-possessing them for Christ. To take them over as they are would be syncretism. 'Re-possession', on the other hand, entails four steps: (a) the selection of certain elements from one's culture; (b) the rejection of other elements which are incompatible with the essence of the biblical faith; (c) the purification from the elements selected and adopted of everything unworthy; (d) the integration of these into the faith and life of the Church.

The age to come has broken into this present age in such a way as to touch our lives with both grace and judgment. It cuts through every culture. Vatican II referred to this discontinuity, and also emphasized the need for 'the spiritual qualities and endowments of every age and nation' to be fortified, completed and restored in Christ.[33]

For Jesus Christ is lord of all, and our supreme desire vis à vis each culture is to 'take every thought captive to obey Christ' (2 Cor. 10:5).

7
The Possibilities of Common Witness

7

The Possibilities of Common Witness

We turn in our last chapter from theological exploration to practical action. We have indicated where we agree and disagree. We now consider what we can do and cannot do together. Since our discussion on this topic was incomplete, what follows awaits further development.

(i) Our Unity and Disunity

We have tried to face with honesty and candour the issues which divide us as Roman Catholics and Evangelicals. We have neither ignored, nor discounted, nor even minimized them. For they are real, and in some cases serious.

At the same time, we know and have experienced that the walls of our separation do not reach to heaven. There is much that unites us, and much in each other's different manifestations of Christian faith and life which we have come to appreciate. Our concern throughout our dialogue has not been with the structural unity of churches, but rather with the possibilities of common witness. So when we write of 'unity', it is this that we have in mind.

To begin with, we acknowledge in ourselves and in each other a firm belief in God, Father, Son and Holy Spirit. This faith is for us more than a conviction; it is a commitment. We have come to the Father through the Son by the Holy Spirit (Eph. 2:18).

We also recognize that the gospel is God's good news about his Son Jesus Christ (Rom. 1:1–3), about his godhead and manhood, his life and teaching, his acts and promises, his death and resurrection, and about the salvation he has once accomplished and now offers. Moreover, Jesus Christ is our Saviour and our Lord, for he is the object of our personal trust, devotion and expectation. Indeed, faith, hope and love are his gifts to us, bestowed on us freely without any merit of our own.

In addition, God's Word and Spirit nourish this new life within us. We see in one another 'the fruit of the Spirit', which is 'love, joy, peace, patience, kindness, goodness, faithfulness, gentleness, and self-control' (Gal. 5:22, 23). No wonder Paul continues in this text with an exhortation that there be among us 'no self-conceit, no provoking of one another, no envy of one another' (v.26).

There is therefore between us an initial if incomplete unity.

Nevertheless, divisions continue, even in some doctrines of importance, as we have made clear in earlier chapters of our report. Our faith has developed in us strong convictions (as it should), some uniting us, others dividing us. The very strength of our convictions has not only drawn us together in mutual respect, but has also been a source of painful tension. This has been the price of our encounter; attempts to conceal or dilute our differences would not have been authentic dialogue, but a travesty of it. So would have been any attempt to magnify or distort our differences. We confess that in the past members of both our constituencies have been guilty of misrepresenting each other, on account of either laziness in study, unwillingness to listen, superficial judgments or pure prejudice. Whenever we have done this, we have borne false witness against our neighbour.

This, then, is the situation. Deep truths already unite us in

Christ. Yet real and important convictions still divide us. In the light of this, we ask: what can we do together?

(ii) Common Witness

'Witness' in the New Testament normally denotes the unique testimony of the apostolic eyewitnesses who could speak of Jesus from what they had seen and heard. It is also used more generally of all Christians who commend Christ to others out of their personal experience of him, and in response to his commission. We are using the word here, however, in the even wider sense of any Christian activity which points to Christ, a usage made familiar by the two documents, jointly produced by the World Council of Churches and the Roman Catholic Church, which are entitled *Common Witness and Proselytism* (1970) and *Common Witness* (1980).

(a) Common witness in Bible translation and publishing

It is extremely important that Roman Catholics and Protestants should have an agreed, common text in each vernacular. Divergent texts breed mutual suspicion; a mutually acceptable text develops confidence and facilitates joint Bible study. The United Bible Societies have rendered valuable service in this area, and the Common Bible (R.S.V.) published in English in 1973, marked a step forward in Roman Catholic-Protestant relationships.

The inclusion of the Old Testament Apocrypha (books written in Greek during the last two centuries before Christ), which the Roman Catholic Church includes as part of the Bible, has proved a problem, and in some countries Evangelicals have for this reason not felt free to use this version. The United Bible Societies and the Secretariat for Promoting Christian Unity have published some guidelines in this matter,[34] which recommend that the Apocrypha be printed 'as a separate section before the New Testament' and described as 'deutero-canonical'. Many Evangelicals feel able to use a Common Bible in these circumstances, although most would prefer the Apocrypha to be omitted altogether.

(b) Common witness in the use of media

Although we have put down the availability of a Common Bible as a priority need, Evangelicals and Roman Catholics are united in recognizing the importance of Christian literature in general, and of Christian audio-visual aids. In particular, it is of great value when the Common Bible is supplemented by common Bible reading aids. In some parts of the world Bible atlases and handbooks, Bible dictionaries and commentaries, and explanatory notes for daily Bible reading, are available in a form which betrays no denominational or ecclesiastical bias. The same is true of some Christian films and filmstrips. So Evangelicals and Roman Catholics may profitably familiarize themselves with each other's materials, with a view to using them whenever possible.

In addition, the opportunity is given to the churches in some countries to use the national radio and television service for Christian programmes. We suggest, especially in countries where Christians form a small minority of the total population, that the Roman Catholic Church, the Protestant Churches and specialist organizations cooperate rather than compete with one another in the development of suitable programmes.

(c) Common witness in community service

The availability of welfare varies greatly from country to country. Some governments provide generous social services, although often the spiritual dimension is missing, and then Christians can bring faith, loving compassion and hope to an otherwise secular service. In other countries the government's provision is inadequate or unevenly distributed. In such a situation the churches have a particular responsibility to discover the biggest gaps and seek to fill them. In many cases the government welcomes the Church's contribution.

In the name of Christ, Roman Catholics and Evangelicals can serve human need together, providing emergency relief for the victims of flood, famine and earthquake, and shelter for refugees; promoting urban and rural development; feeding the hungry and healing the sick; caring for the elderly and the dying; providing a marriage guidance, enrichment and reconciliation service, a pregnancy advisory service and support for single parent families; arranging educational opportunities for the illiterate and job creation schemes for the unemployed; and rescuing young people from drug addiction and young women from prostitution. There seems to be no justification for organizing separate Roman Catholic and Evangelical projects of a purely humanitarian nature, and every reason for undertaking them together. Although faith may still in part divide us, love for neighbour should unite us.

(d) Common witness in social thought and action

There is a pressing need for fresh Christian thinking about the urgent social issues which confront the contemporary world. The Roman Catholic Church has done noteworthy work in this area, not least through the social encyclicals of recent Popes. Evangelicals are only now beginning to catch up after some decades of neglect. It should be to our mutual advantage to engage in Christian social debate together. A clear and united Christian witness is needed in face of such challenges as the nuclear arms race, North-South economic inequality, the environmental crisis, and the revolution in sexual mores.

Whether a common mind will lead us to common action will depend largely on how far the government of our countries is democratic or autocratic, influenced by Christian values or imbued with an ideology unfriendly to the gospel. Where a regime is oppressive, and a Christian prophetic voice needs to be heard, it should be a single voice which speaks for both Roman Catholics and Protestants. Such a united witness could also provide some stimulus to the quest for peace, justice and disarmament; testify to the sanctity of sex, marriage and family life; agitate for the reform of permissive abortion legislation; defend human rights and religious freedom, denounce the use of torture, and campaign for prisoners of conscience; promote Christian moral values in public life and in the education of children; seek to eliminate racial and sexual discrimination; contribute to the renewal of decayed inner cities; and oppose dishonesty and corruption. There are many such areas in which Roman Catholics and Evangelicals can both think together and take action together. Our witness will be stronger if it is a common witness.

(e) Common witness in dialogue

The word 'dialogue' means different things to different people. Some Christians regard it as inherently compromising, since they believe it expresses an unwillingness to affirm revealed truth, let alone to proclaim it. But to us 'dialogue' means a frank and serious conversation between individuals or groups, in which each side is prepared to listen respectfully to the other, with a view to increased understanding on the part of both. We see no element of compromise in this. On the contrary, we believe it is essentially Christian to meet one another face to face, rather than preserving our isolation from one another and even indifference to one another, and to listen to one another's own statements of position, rather than relying on second-hand reports. In authentic dialogue we struggle to listen carefully not only to what the other person is saying, but to the strongly cherished concerns which lie behind his or her words. In this process our caricatures of one another become corrected.

We believe that the most fruitful kind of Evangelical—Roman Catholic dialogue arises out of joint Bible study. For, as this report makes clear, both sides regard the Bible as God's Word, and acknowledge the need to read, study, believe and obey it. It is surely through the Word of God that, illumined by the Spirit of God, we shall progress towards greater agreement.

We also think that there is need for Evangelical—Roman Catholic dialogue on the great theological and ethical issues which are being debated in all the churches, and that an exchange of visiting scholars in seminaries could be particularly productive.

Honest and charitable dialogue is beneficial to those who take part in it; it enriches our faith, deepens our understnding, and fortifies and clarifies our convictions. It is also a witness in itself, inasmuch as it testifies to the desire for reconciliation and meanwhile expresses a love which encompasses even those who disagree.

Further, theological dialogue can sometimes lead to common

affirmation, especially in relation to the unbelieving world and to new theological trends which owe more to contemporary culture than to revelation or Christian tradition. Considered and united declarations by Roman Catholics and Evangelicals could make a powerful contribution to current theological discussion.

(f) Common witness in worship
The word 'worship' is used in a wide range of senses from the spontaneous prayers of the 'two or three' met in Christ's name in a home to formal liturgical services in church.

We do not think that either Evangelicals or Roman Catholics should hesitate to join in common prayer when they meet in each other's homes. Indeed, if they have gathered for a Bible study group, it would be most appropriate for them to pray together for illumination before the study and after it for grace to obey. Larger informal meetings should give no difficulty either. Indeed, in many parts of the world Evangelicals and Roman Catholics are already meeting for common praise and prayer, both in charismatic celebrations and in gatherings which would not describe themselves thus. Through such experiences they have been drawn into a deeper experience of God and so into a closer fellowship with one another. Occasional participation in each other's services in church is also natural, especially for the sake of family solidarity and friendship.

It is when the possibility of common participation in the Holy Communion or Eucharist is raised, that major problems of conscience arise. Both sides of our dialogue would strongly discourage indiscriminate approaches to common sacramental worship.

The Mass lies at the heart of Roman Catholic doctrine and practice, and it has been emphasized even more in Catholic spirituality since the Second Vatican Council. Anyone is free to attend Mass. Other Christians may not receive Communion at it, however, except when they request it in certain limited cases of 'spiritual necessity' specified by current Roman Catholic legislation. Roman Catholics may on occasion attend a Protestant Communion service as an act of worship. But there is no ruling of the Roman Catholic Church which would permit its members to receive Communion in a Protestant Church service, even on ecumenical occasions. Nor would Roman Catholics feel in conscience free to do so.

Many Evangelical churches practise an 'open' Communion policy, in that they announce a welcome to everybody who 'is trusting in Jesus Christ for salvation and is in love and charity with all people', whatever their church affiliation. They do not exclude Roman Catholic believers. Most Evangelicals would feel conscientiously unable to present themselves at a Roman Catholic Mass, however, even assuming they were invited. This is because the doctrine of the Mass was one of the chief points at issue during the sixteenth century Reformation, and Evangelicals are not satisfied with the Roman Catholic explanation of the relation between the sacrifice of Christ on the cross and the sacrifice of the Mass. But this question was not discussed at our meetings.

Since both Roman Catholics and Evangelicals believe that the Lord's Supper was instituted by Jesus as a means of grace,[35] and agree that he commanded his disciples to 'do this in remembrance' of him, it is a grief to us that we are so deeply divided in an area in which we should be united, and that we are therefore unable to obey Christ's command together. Before this becomes possible, some profound and sustained theological study of this topic will be needed; we did not even begin it at ERCDOM.

(g) *Common witness in evangelism*

Although there are some differences in our definitions of evangelism, Roman Catholics and Evangelicals are agreed that evangelism involves proclaiming the gospel, and that therefore any common evangelism necessarily presupposes a common commitment to the same gospel. In earlier chapters of this report we have drawn attention to certain doctrines in which our understanding is identical or very similar. We desire to affirm these truths together. In other important areas, however, substantial agreement continues to elude us, and therefore common witness in evangelism would seem to be premature, although we are aware of situations in some parts of the world in which Evangelicals and Roman Catholics have felt able to make a common proclamation.

Evangelicals are particularly sensitive in this matter, which is perhaps not surprising, since their very appellation 'evangelical' includes in itself the word 'evangel' (gospel). Evangelicals claim to be 'gospel' people, and are usually ready, if asked, to give a summary of their understanding of the gospel. This would have at its heart what they often call 'the finished work of Christ', namely that by bearing our sins on the cross Jesus Christ did everything necessary for our salvation, and that we have only to put our trust in him in order to be saved. Although many Evangelicals will admit that their presentation of the gospel is often one-sided or defective, yet they could not contemplate any evangelism in which the good news of God's justification of sinners by his grace in Christ through faith alone is not proclaimed.

Roman Catholics also have their problems of conscience. They would not necessarily want to deny the validity of the message which Evangelicals preach, but would say that important aspects of the gospel are missing from it. In particular, they emphasize the need both to live out the gospel in the sacramental life of the church and to respect the teaching authority of the Church. Indeed, they see evangelism as essentially a Church activity done by the Church in relation to the Church.

So long as each side regards the other's view of the gospel as defective, there exists a formidable obstacle to be overcome. This causes us particular sorrow in our dialogue on mission, in which we have come to appreciate one another and to discover unexpected agreements. Yet we must respect one another's integrity. We commit ourselves to further prayer, study and discussion in the hope that a way forward may be found.

(iii) Unworthy Witness

We feel the need to allude to the practice of seeking to evangelize people who are already church members, since this causes mis-understanding and even resentment, especially when Evangelicals are seeking to 'convert' Roman Catholics. It arises from the phenomenon which Evangelicals call 'nominal Christianity', and which depends on the rather sharp distinction they draw between the visible Church (of professing or 'nominal' Christians) and the invisible Church (of committed or genuine Christians), that is, between those who are Christian only in name and those who are Christian in reality. Evangelicals see nominal Christians as needing to be won for Christ. Roman Catholics also speak of 'evangelizing' such people, although they refer to them as 'lapsed' or 'inactive' rather than as 'nominal', because they do not make a separation between the visible and invisible Church. They are understandably offended whenever Evangelicals appear to regard all Roman Catholics as *ipso facto* unbelievers, and when they base their evangelism on a distorted view of Roman Catholic teaching and practice. On the other hand, since Evangelicals seek to evangelize the nominal members of their own churches, as well as of others, they see this activity as an authentic concern for the gospel, and not as a reprehensible kind of 'sheep-stealing'. Roman Catholics do not accept this reasoning.

We recognize that conscientious conviction leads some people to change from Catholic to Evangelical or Evangelical to Catholic allegiance, and leads others to seek to persuade people to do so. If this happens in conscience and without coercion, we would not call it proselytism.

There are other forms of witness, however, which we would all describe as 'unworthy', and therefore as being 'proselytism' rather than 'evangelism'. We agree, in general, with the analysis of this given in the study document entitled *Common Witness and Proselytism* (1970), and in particular we emphasize three aspects of it.

First, proselytism takes place when our *motive* is unworthy, for example when our real concern in witness is not the glory of God through the salvation of human beings but rather the prestige of our own Christian community, or indeed our personal prestige.

Secondly, we are guilty of proselytism whenever our *methods* are unworthy, especially when we resort to any kind of 'physical coercion, moral constraint or psychological pressure', when we seek to induce conversion by the offer of material or political benefits, or when we exploit other people's need, weakness or lack of education. These practices are an affront both to the freedom and dignity of human beings and to the Holy Spirit whose witness is gentle and not coercive.

Thirdly, we are guilty of proselytism whenever our *message* includes 'unjust or uncharitable reference to the beliefs or practices of other religious communities in the hope of winning adherents'. If we find it necessary to make comparisons, we should compare the strengths and weaknesses of one church with those of the other, and not set what is best in the one against what is worst in the other. To descend to deliberate misrepresentation is incompatible with both truth and love.

Conclusion

We who have participated in ERCDOM III are agreed that every possible opportunity for common witness should be taken, except where conscience forbids. We cannot make decisions for one another, however, because we recognize that the situation varies in different groups and places. In any case, the sad fact of our divisions on important questions of faith always puts a limit on the common witness which is possible. At one end of the spectrum are those who can contemplate no cooperation of any kind. At the other are those who desire a very full cooperation. In between are many who still find some forms of common witness conscientiously impossible, while they find others to be the natural, positive expression of common concern and conviction. In some Third World situations, for example, the divisions which originated in Europe are felt with less intensity, and mutual trust has grown through united prayer and study of the Word of God. Although all Christians should understand the historical origins and theological issues of the Reformation, yet our continuing division is a stumbling block, and the gospel calls us to repentance, renewal and reconciliation.

We believe that the Evangelical-Roman Catholic Dialogue on Mission has now completed its task. At the same time we hope that dialogue on mission between Roman Catholics and Evangelicals will continue, preferably on a regional or local basis, in order that further progress may be made towards a common understanding, sharing and proclaiming of 'the faith which was once for all delivered to the saints' (Jude 3). We commit these past and future endeavours to God, and pray that by 'speaking the truth in love, we are to grow up in every way into him who is the head, into Christ' (Eph. 4:15).

Appendix: The Meetings and Participants

ERCDOM I (Venice)
April 1977

Evangelical Participants
Professor Peter Beyerhaus
Bishop Donald Cameron
Dr Orlando Costas
Mr Martin Goldsmith
Dr David Hubbard
Rev Gottfried Osei-Mensah
Rev Peter Savage
Rev John Stott

Roman Catholic Participants
Sister Joan Chatfield
Father Pierre Duprey
Monsignor Basil Meeking
Father Dionisio Minguez
    Fernandez
Father John Paul Musinsky
Father Waly Neven
Father Robert Rweyemamu
Father Thomas Stransky

ERCDOM II (Cambridge)
March 1982

Evangelical Participants
Dr Kwame Bediako
Professor Peter Beyerhaus
Bishop Donald Cameron
Mr Martin Goldsmith
Dr David Hubbard
Rev Peter Savage
Rev John Stott
Dr David Wells

Roman Catholic Participants
Sister Joan Chatfield
Father Parmananda Divarkar
Father Pierre Duprey
Father René Girault
Monsignor Basil Meeking
Monsignor Jorge Mejia
Father John Mutiso-Mbinda
Father John Redford
Monsignor Pietro Rossano
Father Thomas Stransky

ERCDOM III (Landévennec)
April 1984

Evangelical Participants
Dr Kwame Bediako
Bishop Donald Cameron
Dr Harvie Conn
Mr Martin Goldsmith
Rev John Stott
Dr David Wells

Roman Catholic Participants
Sister Joan Chatfield
Father Matthieu Collin
Sister Joan Delaney
Father Claude Geffré
Monsignor Basil Meeking
Father Philip Rosato
Bishop Anselme Sanon
Father Bernard Sesboué
Father Thomas Stransky

Endnotes

1 'Evangelism' and 'evangelization' are used indiscriminately in this Report. The former is commoner among Evangelicals, the latter among Roman Catholics, but both words describe the same activity of spreading the gospel.

2 Given the diversity of the Evangelical constituency as well as the differences of understanding between Evangelicals and Roman Catholics, the use of the word 'Church' in this paper inevitably carries some ambiguity. Further conversations would be required before it would be possible to arrive at greater clarity and common terms of ecclesiological discourse.

3 *Decree on Ecumenism (Unitatis Redintegratio)*, 6 in *The Documents of Vatican II*, ed. Walter M Abbott (Geoffrey Chapman 1967)—henceforth *DOV II*.

4 ibid. 4

5 *Dogmatic Constitution on Divine Revelation (Dei Verbum)*, 23, 24 *(DOV II)*.

6 *The Lausanne Covenant:* an exposition and commentary by John Stott (World Wide Publications 1975), Lausanne Occasional Paper No. 3.

7 *Evangelization in the Modern World (Evangelii Nuntiandi)*, Pope Paul VI (Catholic Truth Society 1975).

8 *Lausanne Covenant*, para. 4.

9 *Evangelii Nuntiandi*, 22.

10 e.g. Ps. 19:1–6; Ro. 1:19–20.

11 *Dei Verbum*, 13.

12 *Dei Verbum*, 10.

13 *Dei Verbum*, 22.

14 e.g. 1 Thess. 5:14, 15; Heb. 3:12, 13; 12:15.

15 e.g. Mk. 10:23–27 cf Is. 52:7.

16 In this Report we use 'the Lord's Supper', 'the Holy Communion' and 'the Eucharist' indiscriminately; no particular theology is implied by these terms. 'The Mass' is limited to Roman Catholic contexts. Similarly, we use 'sacrament' or 'ordinance' in relation to Baptism and Eucharist without doctrinal implications.

17 e.g. Eph. 2:1–3; 4:17–19; 2 Cor. 4:3, 4.

18 *Pastoral Constitution on the Church in the Modern World (Gaudium et Spes)*, 13 (*DOV II*).
19 ibid.
20 ibid.
21 Encyclical: *Redemptor Hominis*, Pope John Paul II (Catholic Truth Society 1979), 14.
22 *Dogmatic Constitution on the Church (Lumen Gentium)*, 8 (*DOV II*).
23 *Lumen Gentium*, 16.
24 cf Eph. 3:10; 3:18; 4:13.
25 *Constitution on the Sacred Liturgy (Sacrosanctum Concilium)*, 7, 47 (*DOV II*).
26 e.g. Rom. 4; Gal. 3.
27 *Evangelii Nuntiandi*
28 *Lumen Gentium*, I.
29 Jn. 20:21–22; cf Mt. 28:16–20; Lk. 24:46–49.
30 *The Willowbank Report: Consultation on Gospel and Culture* (Lausanne Committee for World Evangelization 1978), Lausanne Occasional Paper No. 2, para. 2.
31 *Lausanne Covenant*, para. 10.
32 *Decree on the Church's Missionary Activity (Ad Gentes)*, 9 (*DOV II*).
33 *Gaudium et Spes*, 58.
34 *Guiding Principles for Interconfessional Cooperation in Translating the Bible* (1968).
35 see Chapter 4 (3).

DATE DUE